SUFFERING WITH GOD

A thoughtful response on evil, suffering and finding hope
beyond band-aid solutions.

Chris Price

Chris Price

ENDORSEMENTS

"Chris has written a fantastic book on one of the most difficult subjects possible. He has winsomely dealt with the topic; marrying pastoral care, philosophical discernment, cultural application and theological responsibility. A must read book." – Chris Throness, Young Adults Pastor at Coquitlam Alliance Church

"Just because we are saved by God's grace doesn't mean we are exempt from trials and struggles in this world. *Suffering with God* shares some great insights and encouragements that we can hold on to when we are going through valleys in life, and still trust that God is good and is in the struggle with us." – Drago Adam, Owner, The Adam Ad Group

"This book is not only readable but is deeply honest. Rather than shying away from the hard questions concerning evil in our world, it actually expresses the pain and suffering which many of our friends and neighbours feel but sometimes have difficulty articulating. The many illustrations throughout also make it an eminently practical read. Beyond that, the numerous definitions of terms and clarifying of complicated issues will help readers to think clearly about the many facets of this issue. Most importantly, however, this book sets out a number of solutions which show how a God who is both all-powerful and eminently good does not merely coexist with evil but is the ultimate solution to it and hope in the midst of it. This is a book worth reading twice and then passing along to one's neighbours." – Dr. Paul Chamberlain, Trinity Western University & Author of *Why People Don't Believe*

"In *Suffering With God*, Chris Price masters the balance of addressing the questions of our minds without ignoring the feel-

I

ings in our hearts. I have read and re-read this book and found answers to questions of pain and suffering that I have wrestled with my entire life. In the process, I found myself drawn more and more to Jesus, the one who heals our hearts." – Jason Ballard, Host of Alpha's Youth Film Series & Director, Youth Alpha Canada

"With strong arguments, helpful dialogue, inspiring theology and clever stories, Chris Price has provided us with another angle on an important question we all must answer. If you are presently unsure about how you would respond to the question, 'Why does God allow so much suffering and evil?,' I wholeheartedly recommend this book." – Jon Morrison, Associate Director, Apologetics Canada

"What is daddy talking about?" – Kaeden James Price, two-year-old son of author

Chris Price

Suffering With God: A thoughtful response on evil, suffering and finding hope beyond band-aid solutions.

Published By: Apologetics Canada Publishing.
Abbotsford, BC
Canada.

ISBN-13: 978-1494754686

Some names have been changed to protect identities.

ACKNOWLEDGMENTS

This book was a long time coming. First, I would like to thank Jesus for His grace in my life. Thanks to my beautiful wife Diandra and our children Kaeden and Mila. Your love and support allowed me the space to finish this project. To the extended family – I love you all. You are a blessing.

I want to thank Jon Morrison and Andy Steiger from Apologetics Canada for their tireless work. I hope you continue to encourage believers to think and thinkers to believe. Your heart for the church and those outside the church is an inspiration to me.

Thanks to Dr. Paul Chamberlain for his many helpful comments on the early drafts of this book. In fact, a big thanks to anyone who read an early draft of this book and provided feedback (Michelle Felice, Drago Adams and Chris Throness).

I also want to express appreciation to Steve Kroeker and David Smith, who contributed brilliant blogs to this project.

A big shout out to my brilliant editors Judy Baum and Dave Barker, without you this project would be unreadable.

Thanks to Michael Chapman for designing a brilliant cover.

Thanks to Jason Ballard for your feedback, advice, and all around encouragement.

Thanks to Calvary Baptist Church in Coquitlam; staff, church family, friends. I love being on this journey with you.

My hope is that this book brings glory to Christ and much good to you.

Chris Price

Continue the conversation at *sufferingwithgod.com*.

CONTENTS

INTRODUCTION

You are always righteous, Lord, when I bring a case before you. Yet I would speak with you about your justice: Why does the way of the wicked prosper?[1]

Goodness and love are as real as their terrible opposites, and, in truth, far more real...But love is the final reality; and anyone who does not understand this, be he writer or sage, is a man flawed in wisdom.[2]

Why I Write

In 2011, Steve Jobs, the CEO of Apple, the man who brought us the coveted iphone, passed away from cancer. Shortly thereafter, his official biography hit book store shelves across the world. The biography recounts his formative years during which he briefly attended church with his family:

> *Even though they were not fervent about their faith, Jobs' parents wanted him to have a religious upbringing, so they took him to the Lutheran church most Sundays. That came to an end when he was thirteen. In July, 1968, LIFE magazine published a shocking cover showing a pair of starving children in Biafra. Jobs took it to Sunday school and confronted the church's pastor. "If I raise my finger, will God know which one I'm going to raise even before I do it?" The pastor answered, "Yes, God knows everything." Jobs then pulled out the LIFE cover and asked, "Well, does God know about this and what's going to happen to those children?" "Steve, I know you don't understand, but yes, God knows about that." Jobs announced that he didn't want to have anything to do with worshipping such a God, and he never went back to church.[3]*

One of the most influential men in my generation abandoned Christianity because of the problem of evil. I must admit at the outset of this book that I resonate deeply with Steve Jobs' question; I am sure most of us do. Unlike Jobs I have not given up my faith in God but I remain no stranger to occasional bouts of doubt.

Now I find myself as a pastor; both questioning and questioned; both searching for answers to deep inquiries like Jobs, and sought out by others to provide insightful responses to aid them in the midst of existential crises of faith.

More than simply responding to the knotty ambiguities of faith and life, pastoral ministry has caused the problem of evil and suffering to take on a very personal note. This book is birthed partly out of the many tragedies and heartaches I encountered early on in my vocation as a pastor.

There are people I care about with cancer, with failing marriages, with chronic pain and emotional trauma caused by the wicked acts of others. I've married and buried people. I've sat at the bedsides of people struggling to breathe because of a wasting illness. I've held their hands, looked into their eyes, and spoken words of comfort. I've hugged their family members and shed tears with them.

I have a friend whose wife might be leaving him. Of late their home has been flooded with tension, tears and strife. His three-year-old daughter has been putting band-aids all over her body. She knows she hurts, but she can't find the wound. It's heartbreaking to find out at such a young age that there is no BAND-AID for the soul.

The above is just a tiny glimpse into my small sphere of influence. There is a bigger world of wrongdoing outside the walls of my church building. I watch the news some nights and turn away in horror. Murder, dismemberment, rape, theft, child abuse; the list goes on and on. Not to mention the frightening intensity that natural disasters, starvation and disease add to the problem of evil.

In light of such atrocities, to sing sweetly on a Sunday morning, 'This is my Father's world,' seems trite at best, and absurd or stupid at worst. The conflict seems unavoidable and irresolvable; God is perfectly good, God is incredibly powerful, but the people God created suffer horribly. How do Christians hold together these apparently contradictory beliefs without undergoing continual bouts of cognitive dissonance? How do believers tie God's two essential attributes of goodness and power together in their thinking and worship, while the raw data of evil constantly threatens to rip them apart?

More good questions.

For more than half of my life I wasn't a follower of Christ and as a wide-awake citizen of this world I knew about these types of tragedies before I became a Christian. Suffering was part of my pre-conversion data. And unlike Steve Jobs, knowledge of these incidents doesn't shake my faith into shambles, but I do wonder: where is God in all of this mess?

That is the difficult question this book attempts to answer.

The Problem(s) of Evil

The above paragraphs briefly describe some of the real data that contribute to the problem of evil. Evil involves the hurtful action (or inaction) of a personal agent for which that agent is responsible. Moral evil could include horrific acts like murder, rape and physical abuse, or what might be looked upon as 'lesser' evils like slander, lying, or verbal abuse. Although the line is not altogether clear, it can be helpful to distinguish moral evil from natural 'evil' like tornadoes, earthquakes, and wasting diseases.[4] It must be acknowledged at the beginning of our journey together, however, that there is actually more than one problem of evil and different aspects of the problem require different responses. We will follow many thinkers, theologians and philosophers in distinguishing between the intellectual and emotional problem of evil.

Intellectual[5]

The intellectual problem involves reconciling the reality of all this evil with the existence of an all-knowing, all-powerful, all-good God. If God were benevolent He wouldn't want evil to exist; if God were all-powerful He would have the ability to accomplish what He desires. Evil exists so God must lack goodness or power; in other words, God is either wicked or wimpy. The traditional God of the Christian faith, therefore, must not exist. This was Steve Jobs' conclusion; should it be ours?

There are a variety of ways in which one can both state and respond to the intellectual problem of evil and suffering. In the first chapter of this book, however, we will address the logical problem stated above with a focus on the free will defense. The free will defense is a popular response to the intellectual problem of evil, but is it persuasive?

We shall see.

Emotional

Years ago a wonderful woman in our church was diagnosed with terminal cancer. One of our unspoken fears quickly became her living reality. Cancer mercilessly disrupts what takes a lifetime to create; it indiscriminately steals away mothers, fathers, brothers and sisters, and children. Even children. Cancer took her too. After a courageous battle, at times sustained visibly by God's grace, she was gone. This woman faithfully attended our church with a loving husband and two teenage boys who desperately needed a mother. Cancer didn't care.

After hearing the diagnosis, I remember walking into the youth pastor's office at our church; he spun around in his chair, turning to face me with tears streaming down his cheeks. He had just heard the disheartening news and, unfortunately, this wasn't the only heartbreaking story that had crossed his desk that week. Through the tears he asked me a simple, straightforward question, 'Is it always like this?' I assumed, correctly on this occasion, that he was referring to pastoral ministry. My reply was short and to the point. 'Yes,' I said, and the weight of that one word answer settled softly in the room. In a church of several hundred people, ages ranging all the way from the cradle to the grave, it seems as if someone is always struggling with chronic pain, being diagnosed with cancer, or losing a loved one. This is the intractable nature of life lived in community; it can be as comforting as plush cushions and as hard as two-inch nails. Pastoral ministry in such a context is permeated with joy, but it is also constantly tinged by sorrow that, at times, threatens to obscure 'the goodness of God in the land of the living.'[6] This is the emotional problem of evil.

Evil and suffering, for most people, is not a philosophical question, it is a deeply personal problem. This is, in part, why it is crucial to distinguish between the intellectual problem of evil and the emotional problem of evil and provide suitable answers for each. In the words of philosopher Daniel Howard-Snyder, "Many of us are faced with the deterioration of our bodies and minds; we are afraid and in constant, sometimes excruciating, pain; we see our loved ones crushed by cruelty or Nature's firm hand. We need solace, not syllogisms. To be offered philosophical speculations in times like these is to be offered a cold stone when only warm bread will do."[7]

Therefore, in chapters 2, 3 and 4 we will address the emotional and pastoral problem that evil and suffering creates for individuals. In these pages we will intentionally broaden our topic from simply addressing human iniquity to tackling, in a more general fashion, the issue of human suffering by drawing into the conversation several core doctrines of Christianity.

In philosophical discussions surrounding the problem of evil, Christian doctrines are often dropped in favour of a free will defense, or some other type of theodicy (a defense of God's justice in light of wanton human depravity), that engages the skeptic on the common ground of reason and philosophical argumentation. This approach is to be commended in certain circles. It can be counter productive to quote scripture at the philosophical atheist who does not acknowledge the Bible's authority. I appreciate the skilled Christian logicians who meet the atheist and skeptic alike in the arena of academia, and the moderate success they have achieved in defending theism from charges of irrationality. The main burden of this book, however, is to address the emotional, or pastoral, problem of evil by bringing into the conversation the core doctrines of Christianity. If the Christian worldview is being challenged by the problem of evil the Christian may answer with the resources that his or her worldview provides.

So in these chapters we will focus on the uniqueness of Christianity as the only theistic worldview in which the Creator God stepped into creation to suffer with us, for us, and ultimately to take all suffering away from us (Chapter 2). We will also explore the resurrection of Jesus Christ (Chapter 3) and God's promise of a new heavens and a new earth (Chapter 4).

Interspersed throughout the book will be shorter reflections that address in a Biblical manner malicious acts done by people, applying a few of the insights provided by this book to specific situations. This will aid the reader in grasping how the Christian worldview allows us to approach egregious acts of human depravity or suffering in a redemptive, hope-filled manner; training you in your own personal response to traumatic events in our world and in our individual lives. A few of these brief reflections will also offer thought provoking insights about evil, atheism and the Biblical book of Job.

Biblical Omissions

The Christian reader picking up this book may be surprised, however, by the apparent omission of certain Biblical teachings. For example, though I am personally aware that God miraculously heals individuals of all sorts of diseases today, I neglect to explore a theology of healing throughout the course of this short book. Moreover, I have also omitted a full discussion of the early chapters of Genesis and the doctrine of the fall, leaving it for another author to tackle. The fall is a reference to the fact that the first humans freely rebelled against God, toppling themselves from their original status of righteousness.[8] The fall is directly relevant to the problem of evil and I will presuppose its factual reality throughout this work. I refuse, however, to engage in a thorough discussion of it.

I will neglect to explore the connection between humanity's sin and the cursing of the ground and whether or not this led to a fundamentally different physical environment such as the one we experience now. These omissions allow me to avoid all the controversy swirling around the genre of Genesis, the theory of evolution, and the historicity of Adam and Eve. These issues are certainly important but would drag us too far afield, intersecting with areas of study that I'm not prepared to tackle in this short work.

Like most evangelical Christians I am committed to a historic fall, but there are elements in the Garden of Eden that, in my opinion, are metaphorical. For example, 'the tree of the knowledge of good and evil': this tree, I believe, is metaphorical, but it is symbolic of a literal historic choice. In Genesis chapter two we witness the human will at work; to obey or disobey that is the question; a question that is timeless and therefore, always timely. The seeds of every evil act are contained in the precious gift of choice represented by the tree. I believe, as the Bible teaches, that at a certain point in the early days of humanity we chose to rebel against our Maker. A harmful, spiritual mutation occurred in our race's infancy and has spread throughout the entire human genome. An inward curvature of the will, a stubborn autonomy, a bundle of disordered desires; a profound alienation from our creator has plagued our natural state since that fateful day in Eden. But whatever the reader chooses to believe about the early chapters of Genesis, or the interplay between Biblical theology and modern science; we can all agree that the consequences of sin are still with us today making a project like this one painfully necessary.[9]

A Concluding Thought: A Boy and a Band-Aid

It is with fear and trembling that any author would pick up the pen and presume to write on this topic. Silence in the face of suffering is often better than speech; a loving presence more conducive to healing than precise, philosophical propositions. All God-fearing writers who tackle this subject fear an affinity with Job's friends and the thunderous pronouncement of God's disfavor over our particular pile of scribbling. It remains true that in seeking to 'defend' God from charge of wrong doing in the face of evil we can alienate the sufferer by trivializing the evil done to them, or the suffering they have undergone. So let me end this introduction with a true story, transformed into a parable, to again express my purpose and prayer for this book.

My wife and I were recently at a child's second birthday party. It was a warm summer day and the festivities were located in the hosts' spacious backyard. Moments before the birthday cake was unveiled our friends' four year old son tumbled off the trampoline and severely broke his arm. As he writhed on the ground in agony his parents rushed to his side. His mom was understandably distraught. After all, her little boy's arm was bent at an unnatural angle and his anguished cries sounded jarringly loud in the midst of the solemn silence that had descended like a shroud on the party.

I clearly remember this little boy crying out repeatedly for a BAND-AID, because when you are a child and you get hurt a BAND-AID helps make the pain go away. His mom obliged him and with trembling hands gingerly applied a BAND-AID on his cracked and crooked arm as we waited for the ambulance to arrive. "It is not working, it is not working, it is not working," cried out the boy. I can only speculate, but this may have been the first time real, intense pain forced on him the realization that BAND-AIDs don't work for every wound.

Some of you reading this book have suffered greatly. You have been grievously wounded by people in your life. You've out-grown simple solutions, the dark underbelly of life has robbed you of their usefulness.

BAND-AIDs don't mend broken bones.

Logic doesn't lessen the sting of loss.

Answers don't always sooth personal anguish.

This book is not a BAND-AID. This book is not a healer. My hope is that this book is a revealer of the God who, in His time, will do the healing. A God who can reset your soul, strengthen you in your suffering, and make you whole.

We will begin our journey, however, by addressing the logical problem of evil through the free will defense. This is the most common Christian response to our topic and it is directly connected to the fall described in the course of this introduction; but does it succeed at explaining how God and human depravity can co-exist?

Let us find out together.

Chris Price

FREE WILL

CHAPTER ONE

Bedtime Behavior

When our two-year-old son, Kaeden, makes a bad choice his mother and I discipline him. Unfortunately the discipline often leads to a string of terrible decisions on his part as his stubborn will exerts itself against our firm but loving opposition. Several nights ago I was attempting to put him to bed but he was stubbornly refusing to listen to my instructions. I warned him that there would be consequences and when he continued to play deaf I followed through with the promised discipline. Our much-anticipated nightly routine, which my wife and I have affectionately labeled our 'bed party', was cancelled. No reading books, no cuddling, and straight to bed. Sadly, like most discipline enforced by loving parents, it actually felt like more of a punishment for me because I really love those uninterrupted moments of debriefing the day with my son.

On this occasion, my son engaged in a retaliatory response to my disciplinary action. My sweet, little, sinful boy smacked me squarely in the face. Not once, not twice, but repeatedly. The boy we (she) had brought into this world raised his two little fists in willful defiance of my loving, benevolent, bedside dictatorship.

Every parent can relate to a story like this. And so can every child; which pretty much covers everyone alive on planet earth. We have all made bad choices and good choices but one thing is constant: <u>we make choices</u>. To the degree that it is us making the decisions <u>we are accountable</u> for them. When my son punch-

11

es me angrily in the jaw I don't discipline myself, or blame our ancestral gene pool, or his home environment, which is, to be honest, a hit free zone.

Instead, I blame him for his actions, less when he is young, of course, but increasingly more as he matures and grows. Parental discipline aside, our entire judicial system, as broken as it may be, rests on the assumption that the above is still true as we transition into adulthood. And in the end, all discipline, whether parental or judicial, inadvertently brings us face to face with the concept of free will.[1]

What do we Mean by Free Will?[2]

Before we proceed in our discussion, we have to define free will. By 'free will' I am referring to our human ability to act to the contrary in any given situation without our decisions being wholly determined by external, or internal influences. If you glance back on the course of your life many crucial decisions will come to mind that have significantly shaped who you are today. The college you chose to attend, the friends you've invited to speak into your life, the person you decided to marry, and the places you've chosen to call home; these were all key decisions that have greatly influenced the person you've become. The understanding of free will argued for in this chapter requires that in any of these given situations, though your choices were likely influenced by upbringing and other social and psychological factors, you had the ability to make different decisions than the ones you actualized.

The above understanding of freedom is necessary for moral responsibility to be a coherent concept. If our choices are determined for us, we cannot be consistently praised for virtuous acts or condemned for immoral behavior. This is true in regard to my son's hitting and it will remain true as he grows up. For example, if, years down the road, I were to duct-tape my son's mouth shut for unleashing a string of obscenities, it would make little sense for me to return one hour later and lavish praise on my son for learning to bridle his tongue. I left him no choice in the matter; with the duct tape firmly in place he couldn't speak, let alone swear. Moreover, it is worth pointing out to the horrified reader that it would be senseless to accuse me of abusive behavior towards my son if I was unable to act in a contrary manner. Abuse in my past, or stresses in my present life, may have influenced the nature of my disciplinary action, but those external, or internal, factors didn't determine how I behaved to the point where I bear no moral blame for the abusive manner in which I disciplined my boy.

Through this fictitious example we can clearly perceive that free-dom of the will, as defined above, is necessary for moral account-ability and virtuous actions to be meaningful concepts in our so-ciety. And not only does the above concept of freedom allow for moral responsibility, it makes possible genuine love.

We can flush out the truth of this proposition by engaging in another brief thought experiment: Imagine you could mix to-gether a potion that would simulate all the feelings and behaviors normally associated with the experience of being in love. In an attempt to woo the uninterested person of your desire you slip him or her a hefty dose of your love potion. He or she promptly, and happily, falls head over heels 'in love' with you.

You would know, however, that the relationship is a sham. Your partner doesn't really love you; they are being unwillingly and unknowingly subjected to these euphoric feelings by a potion of your own concoction. The relationship is an illusion, a mirage. If the potion isn't administered, the passion won't be reciprocated. Intimacy is imitated but not actually experienced. <u>Genuine intimacy, after all, requires a willingness to open oneself up to another person, risking all the fears associated with potential rejection and putting your heart in the hands of another fallible, flawed person</u>. Love is a risk, but those who experience its embrace and the corresponding delight of authentic intimacy know it is worth the gamble. In this way, <u>love requires free choice</u>.

In a manner similar to human lovers and analogous to a parent training their child in virtue or responsibility, it would be reasonable to assume that if God desired a loving relationship with His creatures, in addition to us developing moral character and responsibility, He would have created us with the type of freedom argued for in the preceding paragraphs. To ask God to create us without this type of freedom would be the equivalent of requesting that God create humans without actually creating humans.

In addition to the above understanding of freedom, how we understand the omnipotence of God is also incredibly relevant to our topic. What does it mean for us to claim that God is all-powerful? Does this divine attribute imply that God can do whatever He wants? Are there some things, or possible worlds, or states of affair, that God can't bring about? We will investigate this crucial issue next.

Free Will & God's Omnipotence

Can God make a burrito so hot that not even He can eat it? A high school student once asked me this question. Here is another: Can God create a stone so heavy that not even He can lift it?

These types of questions, though silly on the surface, get to the heart of what it means, or doesn't mean, for God to be all-powerful, or omnipotent.

Throughout church history the vast majority of theologians have understood God's omnipotence to mean that God can do all things that are intrinsically possible. Though we may be unaware of a vast number of things that may or may not be intrinsically possible, most philosophers are clear that logical contradictions are not possible in any world. A logical contradiction involves two statements that cannot both be true if understood in the same way or referred to at the same time. For example, I cannot be both married and a bachelor at the same time if bachelor means, by definition, an unmarried man. Now, at different times in my life it may have been true to state that I am a bachelor or I am a married man. It can't, however, be true at the same time and in the same sense that I am a married bachelor. That would be a contradiction.

In reference to God, He can do anything that is possible, but contradictions aren't things; they are non-entities, or meaningless combinations of words.[3] God can't perform contradictions. For example, God can't move an immovable object, or bring about a state of affairs where He exists and doesn't exist at the same time and in the same sense.

In addition to contradictions, there are a multitude of things that God cannot do resulting from His very nature. Two notable examples are: God can't sin and God can't cease to exist. God is a perfectly good, necessary Being by definition in Christian theology and if God could lie or cease to exist He wouldn't be God.

Moreover, for those who embrace the Christian scriptures as an authoritative and trustworthy account of God's actions in history, we find that when God makes unconditional promises to His people He has, in a sense, tied His hands because of His faithfulness and unchanging nature - He has committed Himself to one course of action. Of course, in His omnipotence God could have chosen any manner of proceeding, but once He has committed Himself to a particular path He can't go back on it by His very nature. God can't leave unconditional promises made to His people unfulfilled. There is no logical contradiction involved in the above examples, but these scenarios still represent things that God can't do.[4]

The Death of a Thousand Qualifications

The unsympathetic reader may very well wonder how the traditional Christian understanding of God's omnipotence doesn't die the death of a thousand qualifications. Doesn't omnipotence become a meaningless term with all of these qualifiers? God can do anything, but make sure you read the fine print; by anything we don't mean this, that and the other thing.

Though the above objection is understandable, in response it should be pointed out our conceptualization of God's omnipotence isn't left in shambles after the preceding paragraphs.[5] We have only added a few qualifiers to our understanding of omnipotence for the sake of clarity. God's omnipotence means that God can do anything that is intrinsically possible and in accordance with His nature, plans and purposes outlined in scripture.[6]

Omnipotence and the Problem of Evil

Let me remind the reader of our conversation thus far. We have defined freedom as the ability to make decisions in a manner not wholly determined by external or internal influences. Free will is the ability to act to the contrary in any given situation. Then we carefully qualified our understanding of God's omnipotence to match the traditional Christian understanding; God can do all things that are intrinsically possible and in conformity with His nature.

Now, we are ready to ask, 'How do our definition of freedom and our clarified understanding of God's omnipotence relate to the logical problem of evil? After all, if it is true that an all-powerful, all-good, all-knowing God can do anything possible, if He exists, then why couldn't God create a world where no human wickedness exists? And wouldn't His goodness require Him to do so?'

Here is how the free will defender is prone to respond to that objection: As we have admitted above, it is true that God can do anything that is possible, but if we move from that admission to the conclusion that, therefore, evil wouldn't exist, or God doesn't exist, the reasoning is flawed. God cannot give people free will and not give them free will at the same time. That is not possible even for an omnipotent God. That would be a blatant contradiction like God conjuring a square triangle or a married bachelor, or baking bread that He didn't bake.

So if God's desire was to create creatures with freedom to provide space for the greater good of love, virtue, responsibility and worship, evil must be a possibility. If we are free to love, we must be necessarily free to hate. If we possess liberty to serve, we must retain the culpable capability of rebellion.

Here is one more way to think about it: when I first learned to drive I crashed my father's car several times. Needless to say, my dad was not pleased with my poor driving performance; wrecking his car was certainly against his will. Yet, at the same time, it was my father's desire that I learn to drive, which is why he allowed me to borrow his car in the first place. His permission made possible a scenario where his desire for both safe travels and a dent-free fender could be violated. From this simple example we can comprehend how an event can be both against our will and be made possible through an exercise of our will. In a similar manner, evil is against God's will while being made possible by His will.

In this logical framework, supported in many places by scripture, everything God creates is good, and one of the good things God created was freedom. We, however, have misused our freedom to create evil. Sin and evil are against God's moral will, but His permissive will allows it and even uses it, because it makes possible a greater good like love, virtue and worship.

A Critics Response

The critic could respond to the above defense by stating something like the following: Why couldn't God create a world where we all freely choose the good? In this possible world freedom is maintained and wickedness is avoided; it is the ultimate win/win scenario. This must have been a live option for God, otherwise the Christian would be admitting that human depravity is somehow necessary, which has devastating implications for God's goodness.

Is there some type of contradiction involved in saying that God created people so that we would freely choose the good? On the surface there doesn't seem to be an explicit contradiction, so why wouldn't an all-powerful God do this? If God were all good and all powerful He should have created this obviously better world without sin, evil and suffering. He clearly didn't exercise this option, so, as the critic would conclude, God must lack power or goodness. Therefore, the traditional God of Christian belief doesn't exist.

Once we subject the above proposal to serious scrutiny, however, it becomes clear that there is a serious problem with this option sleeping silently below the surface. To be clear, the person who put forwards the above criticism is not contending that God forces us to freely choose. That would be a blatant contradiction. The skeptic's proposal is logically possible, but the unavoidable problem arises when we ask the question, how can God make this world if His desire is that people have genuine free will? How can God guarantee that people won't abuse their free will without taking it away? It is possible that in any world that God created with significantly free creatures we would have gone wrong in the exercise of our freedom. The only way God could, with certainty, avoid the abuse of free will is to take it away completely, or intervene every time we misused our will which amounts to the same thing.

So the above proposal of a possible world better than our current one is, on closer inspection, guilty of misusing the term 'freely'. If God is going to guarantee that we always choose the good, in the end, 'freely' becomes what we are programmed or determined by God to do and, therein, lies the implicit contradiction. This, of course, is not genuine freedom.

What about Heaven?

If the reader has followed the course of the argument this far another objection may have arisen in your mind. Throughout the course of this chapter we repeatedly stated that freedom is required for loving relationships to exist, yet in heaven we will be free and still able to love, but unable to sin; so there is a possible world where we are free to love, but not free to sin. In fact, this concept is central to Christianity. One day we will have a higher freedom; not freedom to sin, but freedom from sin – a God-like type of freedom.

Why didn't God start with that option? The Christian philosopher Norman Geisler writes insightfully in response to this question:

> *In short, God had to create free creatures who could sin before He could produce free creatures who can't sin. It's like the difference between a shotgun wedding and a marriage freely chosen. In both cases the person is married, but in only one case was it free....Since God by His very nature (love) cannot force anyone to love Him, it would be highly improper to think of a heaven where people were forced to be there. First there must be courtship, and then two can be bound together for life.*[7]

Death and eternity is not the time for choosing, as C.S. Lewis once wisely pointed out;[8] it is the moment for discovering what we have already chosen. At death, our choices are solidified, the trajectory of our life on earth is consummated; our sin is burnt up and in God's final purifying fire; our will is granted a higher freedom that we have only flirted with during our earthly journey. We are no longer free to sin, we are free from sin; liberated fully and finally to swim in the waves of mutual love without the undertow of our sinful nature constantly threatening to drag us back into the sea of self.

In the end, God desires a marriage with His people not a staged play with His puppets; a people in love not a people coerced from above; God is a romancer not a rapist, a people pursuer not a computer programmer. God won't trade matrimony for a marionette. So on earth we must be free to love or hate, because for love to be meaningful requires a certain amount of self-determination. This is no longer the case in heaven. Our choices have been made. The wedding has taken place, the relationship has been consummated. We are bound to Him as He is bound to us for all eternity.

Tying It All Together

Once we have understood the value of free will and grasped God's omnipotence properly, we can comprehend how God's goodness and power is compatible with the existence of moral evil. God has chosen to make room for the free choice of His creatures. In granting humanity this freedom of will, moral evil is not necessary, but it is a possibility that humanity actualized through our sin and rebellion.

In the end God does not directly cause evil but He permits it for a time in light of His ultimate goal of having a meaningful love relationship with His creatures, in addition to producing virtue and other related good. The greatest of this good, which has gone unmentioned thus far in this chapter, comes to fruition in the glorification of God's Son magnified exponentially to the world through the salvation of sinners.

The use of our free will to rebel results in the use of God's higher freedom to willingly rescue sinners from themselves, thereby radiating throughout the heavenly places the brilliance and beauty of His mercy and grace. Since all of creation exists to display the glorious nature of God's attributes, moral evil provides an opportunity like no other to put on display the condescending nature of God's mercy, the extravagant nature of His efficacious love, and the gratuitous nature of His redeeming grace for ill-deserving sinners.

Does Freedom Explain Evil?

The free will defense is the most common Christian approach to addressing the problem of evil. But does it succeed? To a point it certainly does shed some light on possible reasons that God may have for permitting evil in our world. Apart from genuine freedom, the greatest good that makes our lives meaningful would vanish into thin air. On the other hand, it is more difficult to see how terrible diseases and natural tragedies can be adequately addressed by a free will defense (see Appendix 1 on Natural Evils).

Moreover, the free will defender tends to use the language of God 'allowing' unrighteousness for His greater purposes. For those Christians who are seeking to think Biblically, however, God allowing evil is a minute category in scripture that is dwarfed by the amount of texts referring to God sending calamity as judgment for sin, or God being ultimately responsible for everything that occurs in His creation. This, of course, doesn't impugn God for every act of human evil. As D.A. Carson writes:

> *God stands behind evil in such a way that not even evil takes place outside the bounds of His sovereignty, yet the evil is not morally chargeable to Him: it is always chargeable to secondary agents, to secondary causes....if this sounds just a bit too convenient for God, my initial response (though there is more to be said) is that according to the Bible this is the only God there is. There is no other.*[9]

Lastly, a free will defense is not much help in the face of tragedy. Is it not insensitive and trite to speak about free will in the hospital room of a person dying from cancer, or at a roadside memorial grieving the loss of a young person? It is striking that the Bible itself never engages in a free will defense in the face of human depravity and decadence. The Biblical book of Job doesn't seem, even on the surface, to glance in the direction of free will to explain Job's trials. Freedom of the will (in some manner or another) appears to be presupposed through the narrative of scripture, held in tension with a robust view of God's sovereignty over all of creation, but, in the face of grievous sin and evil (moral or natural), the scripture's response is not to appeal to a free will defense. It seems we need more than philosophical propositions to confront evil and suffering with courage, dignity and hope; a lifeline from God rather than logic from philosophers.

The Boy with the BAND-AID

Earlier in this book I relayed the story of a young boy who accidentally tumbled off a trampoline severely breaking his arm. In that moment he cried out, pleading with his mom to give him a BAND-AID to take away the pain. Time accomplished what the BAND-AID could not, as the broken bone slowly began to mend. Later x-rays revealed that his arm did not heal properly. As a result, the doctor was forced to re-break the bone so that it could be reset. Apart from this drastic remedial act the little boy would likely have trouble with his right arm for years to come, diminishing his quality of life.

From the perspective of a four-year-old, his parents and the doctor are imposing on him unjust, unnecessary, pointless evil by intentionally breaking his arm again. A small child doesn't have the cognitive capacity, or accumulative life experience, to comprehend his parents' purposes in causing him to undergo such a procedure. Yet, from our grown-up perspective, we know that the parents and the doctor were not evil; they had a morally sufficient reason to re-break the child's arm.

The distance separating the child's intellectual capacities and his parents' is, of course, insignificant contrasted with the yawning chasm dividing God's understanding and our own. Philosopher William Alston mentions seven ways that God's knowledge differs from human beings due to our: lack of data, complexity far beyond what we can handle, severe difficulty in knowing what is metaphysically impossible, ignorance of the wide range of possibilities, ignorance of the range of values (or the various good that would be eliminated alongside God removing any given evil act), and the limits of our ability to make well-informed judgments.[10]

The broken arm story, coupled with Alston's observations, imply that the answer to 'why God allows this or that evil' may, in the end, be far beyond our intellectual pay grade. Free will can potentially help unravel some of the mystery without exhausting the extent of it.[11] So the question then becomes, in light of the amount and atrocious nature of many evils that seemingly defy our comprehension, do we still possess adequate reasons to trust God in the midst of them? What other resources are available from within the Christian worldview to address, in a redemptive fashion, the problem of human wickedness thereby providing confidence for the believer that God is indeed good?

Back to the Bedside

At the beginning of this chapter I recounted how my son smacked me in the face when I lovingly disciplined him. How did I respond to his overt hostility in that moment? I had options. I could have left the room, raised my voice, stolen his blanket in petty payback, or grabbed his hands so that he couldn't strike me again. Instead, I tried something entirely different. As he angrily struck me in the face I repeatedly whispered to him, 'Daddy loves you.' Smack, smack, 'Daddy loves you.' Smack. 'Daddy loves you.' Eventually, he exhausted himself and stopped; he settled down and went quiet. Then I kissed him on the forehead, told him I loved him, and left the room.

Central to the Christian story is a cross; an emblem of suffering that Jesus transformed into a surprising symbol of love and hope. Something about this experience with my son reminded me of Jesus on the cross; His own creation beating Him and bruising Him, yet his long-suffering love still willing to extend forgiveness and grace.

I pictured Jesus getting repetitively punched and brutally beaten to a bloody pulp and nailed up on a cruel cross; helplessly hanging there, but still spreading His arms to God's wayward world whispering softly, 'I love you this much.' 'I love you.' Smack. 'I love you.' Smack, smack. All the while hopeful that we will exhaust ourselves from our own sinful striving and collapse peaceably into God's proverbial arms again; quiet and at rest in His loving kindness and unearned favour.

The cross of Christ is what I reflected on that night my own son decided to use me as a punching bag. And in the next chapters of this book we will examine the person and work of Jesus, which, I believe, will give us concrete grounds for affirming: yes, God is still good in a world gone bad.

Quote For Reflection:

Suffering can produce good fruit in our lives. It is important to keep in mind, however, that suffering is not a good thing in and of itself. Suffering should not be pursued, but resisted and alleviated wherever found. Jesus healed the sick and alleviated sickness and we should seek to do the same. Suffering never saved anyone. Suffering is not redemptive in and of itself. 'What about the sufferings of Jesus?' one might ask. Let us be clear: It was not Jesus' suffering alone that saved; it was the meaning attached to that suffering by God and the first Christians (He suffered for our sins); meaning that was only imputed to His death because of His resurrection.

EVIL AND ATHEISM

*In a universe of blind physical forces and genetic repli-
cation, some people are going to get hurt, other people
are going to get lucky and you won't find any rhyme or
reason in it, nor any justice. The universe as we observe
it has precisely the properties we should expect if there
is, at the bottom, no design, no purpose, no evil and no
good. Nothing but blind, pitiless, indifference. DNA neither knows nor cares. DNA just is. We dance to its music.*
— *Richard Dawkins*

Social Darwinism?

'Science flies rockets to the moon! Religion flies planes into
buildings!' This mantra has inspired many enthusiastic atheists
because it seems to succinctly summarize the underlying foun-
dation of their worldview: 'Science good – religion bad!' The
trouble, however, has never been science or religion. The problem is people.

Our common predicament is produced by human hearts that
can clutch greedily at any ideology or worldview and aggressively employ it as a means of oppressing other people. Science, as
well as religion, has been co-opted by wicked men for wicked
purposes and nowhere is that more clear than when discussing
Social Darwinism. Social Darwinism is the application of Darwinian principles to sociology and ethics. *The Merriam Webster
dictionary* defines Social Darwinism as:

27

An extension of Darwinism to social phenomena; specifically: a sociological theory that socio-cultural advance is the product of inter-group conflict and competition and the socially elite classes (those possessing wealth and power) possess biological superiority in the struggle for existence.

This ideology motivated movements like Eugenics, Scientific Racism, Imperialism, and Nazism. Not surprisingly, this tragic abuse of Darwin's theory of evolution is despicable according to many atheistic thinkers. Prominent philosopher of science, Michael Ruse, explains the inner logic of Social Darwinism in this manner:

One ferrets out the nature of the evolutionary process – the mechanism or cause of evolution – and then one transfers it to the human realm, arguing that that which holds as a matter of fact among organisms holds as a matter of obligation among humans.[12]

In nature, the strong prey on the weak (think *The Hunger Games* on hyper-drive). Nature is violent and harsh and only the strongest pass on their genes to future generations. Therefore, strong primates can oppress the weak with the end result being the less fit races are weeded out. This is part of the evolutionary struggle for survival and it can lead logically to racism and oppression when applied to the human sphere of social interactions.[13]

'Ought' From An 'Is'?

In the late 19th century and early 20th, Some scholars promoted Social Darwinism as a moral imperative, or the advancement of the human species as a moral imperative and Social Darwinism as the means. This approach to ethics led to horrors like forced sterilization, a Nazi ethic, and other such evils. These practitioners were engaging in a leap from 'fact' to 'value'; from what 'is' to what 'ought' to be.[14] Most atheists reject this type of logical move from biology to ethics - from 'is' to 'ought' - when used to prop up and provide legitimacy for Social Darwinism.

In fact, this type of reasoning embodies a mistake that is so common it has an official title, the Naturalistic Fallacy. This fallacy occurs when a person moves from a seemingly accurate description of reality (is) to a morally obligatory prescription about reality (ought).

This concept can be difficult to grasp so allow me to provide a simple example. Examine this statement: If I press this button that bomb will detonate killing those innocent people. Now, let's say that the above description of the situation is accurate; if a red button is pushed countless innocent people will die. For most people this is a great reason for why they should refrain from pushing the button. For others, however, the above statement may provide strong motivation as to why they ought to push the button. Perhaps those innocent people belong to an ethnicity you despise, or you are out for revenge against a certain people group, and these individuals, in your thinking at least, are guilty by racial association and worthy of death.

Here is the point: there is no moral prescription contained within the accurate description of what will occur if that red button is pushed, the morality, the sense of 'ought' and 'ought not', has to come from elsewhere.

The above example clearly shows that simply moving from a description to a prescription, or from an 'is' to an 'ought,' represents a logical misstep, one that is noticed by more than just religious thinkers. As the famous skeptic David Hume added centuries ago, to move from 'is' to 'ought' is a misguided bit of reasoning because nature provides conflicting moral signals and, more devastatingly, the proponent of this misstep is confounding first order (studying nature) and second order (value judgment) activities, thereby engaging in a blatant category mistake.[15]

Evil

How do the above paragraphs relate to the problem of evil? Simply stated, to press the problem of evil against the Christian it seems as though the atheist has to make an illogical leap similar to the one being made by the advocate of Social Darwinism. An act is evil when it 'ought' not to take place. Why is it wrong, evil and wicked for human beings to destroy little children? It ought not to be done, and not simply because it is personally distasteful to me, or even solely because our society disapproves. After all, not all societies have denounced atrocious evils like the destruction of innocent children, so we need a moral standard overarching all cultures, providing a coherent basis for the intrinsic value of human beings by which we can call these cultures to account for their moral blind spots and human rights violations.

To adjudicate between good and evil we require an objective moral standard that atheism fails to provide. This doesn't imply, of course, that the atheist can't discover, or do, that which is morally praiseworthy, but rather that their worldview can't provide a basis for objective good or evil. For example, in the evolutionary scenario both cruelty and kindness can promote the survival of a species and as a result have evolutionary value, but evolution fails to provide us with an objective moral reason for choosing kindness over cruelty.

To say it another way, "Evil as a value judgment marks a departure from some standard of moral perfection. But if there is no standard, there is no departure."[16] In a Godless universe there is no standard of perfection, what then is evil? Given atheism, if nature is all there is, how can we derive any 'ought' or 'ought not' from it?

Two More Possible Problems

In addition, given atheism, morality must have evolved. Yet, if morality evolved morality must have changed, and who can claim that morality has finished evolving? Today's evil may be tomorrow's good, or vice versa, granting us, for only a tiny moment of geological time, a flimsy basis from which to make moral denunciations, as well as offering no accounting, consistent with the atheistic, evolutionary worldview, for the 'ought' and 'ought not' that our ethical experience imposes on us.

Moreover, granting a godless worldview, how can we even speak meaningfully about moral progress? Doesn't moral progress require some kind of objective moral good to which our behavior is progressing closer and closer - a moral law that stands outside of nature but to which our nature is moving inexorably nearer and nearer to reflecting. C.S. Lewis says it well in his essay, *The Poison of Subjectivism*:

> *If good is a fixed point, it is at least possible that we should get nearer and nearer to it; but if the terminus is as mobile as a train, how can the train progress towards it? Our ideas of good may change, but they cannot change either for the better or the worse if there is no absolute and immutable good to which they can approximate or from which they can recede.*[17]

In simpler terms, good can't be a fixed point unless it is rooted in the unchanging nature of God, but it is this God that the atheist denies. In a materialistic, time-and-chance universe to talk of moral progress is pure fantasy. Yet we do speak meaningfully about moral progress so, perhaps, it is atheism that is pure fantasy.

Running Aground

In the end, if all atheism can supply us with is an evolving, relativistic accounting of right and wrong, any argument moving from evil to the nonexistence of God will run aground on the shallowness of the atheist's worldview. If the very concept of evil is relative - a descriptive term that we've been 'taught' by evolutionary pressures and our culture and upbringing to apply to certain actions, but lacking any objectivity in our world - one person's (or culture's) evil could be another person's (culture's) good, and we would possess no transcendent standard to determine who is right and who is wrong. If this were an accurate description of our plight, the logical problem of evil could simply be solved by denying the evil. It can be argued (in a rather obvious manner) that we can't deny the evil so, I believe, we must deny the truth of atheism; again, not in spite of evil, but because of it.

The Final Inconsistency

To come full circle, let me pose this question: Why is the fallacious reasoning from 'is' to 'ought' protested against vehemently (and rightly) by atheists when the horrors and missteps of Social Darwinism are propped up as a moral imperative, but is considered sound reasoning when employed to press the problem of evil? Is it because in one instance the atheist is defending Darwinism and in the other they are attacking God?

I wonder.

The End of the Matter

If the outline of the argument sketched above can be made with greater sophistication and detail (and it can be), including responses to potential objections (i.e. other fallacious attempts to move from 'is' to 'ought'), it may suggest a stunning irony: <u>The atheist's greatest argument against God (evil) requires the existence of God as the ultimate source of objective morality for its legitimacy</u>. In this particular case the atheist may need God to attack theism, thereby showing forth the insufficiency of atheism. C.S. Lewis said it better than I years ago:

> *My argument against God was that the universe seemed so cruel and unjust. But how had I got this idea of "just" and "unjust"?...What was I comparing this universe with when I called it unjust?...Of course I could have given up my idea of justice by saying it was nothing but a private idea of my own. But if I did that, then my argument against God collapsed too - for the argument depended on saying that the world really was unjust, not simply that it did not happen to please my private fancies...Consequently atheism turns out to be too simple.[18]*

Quotes For Reflection

> *[Given atheism] God need not be reconciled to evil, because neither exists. Therefore the problem of evil is no problem at all....And of course since there is no evil, the materialist must, ironically, not use the problem of evil to justify atheism. The problem of evil presupposes the existence of objective evil – the very thing the materialist*

[atheist] seems to deny. The argument that led to materialism is exhausted just when it is needed most. In other words, the problem of evil is generated only by the prior claim that evil exists.[19]

Aggressive apologists for atheism want the Christian to surrender their belief in God in light of genocide. I understand. That type of mass violence makes it hard to believe in God. But it makes it far more difficult to have faith in atheism. A competent scientist won't abandon a theory until a better explanation presents itself. Why, therefore, should a Christian surrender their belief in God for atheism, when it struggles strenuously to provide a coherent reason for condemning genocide that is logically consistent with its supposedly superior worldview? The Christian condemns any and every genocide in the strongest terms because each person, regardless of race or ethnicity, is made in the image of God and thereby possesses objective value and worth. The believer can also speak meaningfully about moral progress as the rights and dignity of people become more fully appreciated in any given culture. Not to be unduly harsh, but that same option doesn't seem to be open to the consistent atheist.[20]

Chris Price

A CHRISTIAN'S CONSOLATION

CHAPTER 2

In the book, *Disappointment with God*, author Philip Yancey shares this unsettling story,

> *It is a peculiarly twentieth-century story, and it is almost too awful to tell: about a boy of twelve or thirteen who, in a fit of crazy anger and depression, got a hold of a gun somewhere and fired it at his father, who died not right away but soon afterward. When the authorities asked the boy why he had done it, he said that it was because he could not stand his father, because his father demanded too much of him, because he hated his father. And then later on, after he had been placed in a house of detention somewhere, a guard was walking down the corridor late one night when he heard sounds from the boy's room, and he stopped to listen. The words that he heard the boy sobbing out in the dark were, "I want my father, I want my father."*[1]

This parable, written originally by Frederick Buechner, is symbolic of one of the underlying assumptions prevalent in the last three chapters of this short book. In a tragic irony so indicative of the modern world of thought, many have tried to use the existence of evil to kill belief in the only Father who can ultimately help us in our time of need.

There is no ultimate consolation for suffering that results from depraved actions in the atheistic worldview. We can, of course, give our suffering whatever meaning we bravely create, but, in the end, it is ultimately meaningless like everything else. The sun will one day gobble up all sin, suffering and salvation leaving only eternal silence and infinite emptiness.

There is no God to make things right; there is no moral arch to the universe that gravitates towards justice (whatever we define justice to be); there is no cosmic embrace, only a cosmic abortion; the atheist has murdered God and tried to resurrect hope, but that type of resurrection would require a miracle and the atheist can't permit one. This is no advancement in thought; it is a tragedy greater than any evil. So is there a better joy producing and hope sustaining option?[2]

The last three chapters of this book will answer that crucial question with an empathic 'yes' by focusing on the God who descends to meet us in our suffering. The Christian worldview, when fully embraced, provides profound comfort and consolation for those who suffer. And while many have testified to an overwhelming experience of God's nearness in the midst of tragedy, the Christian response to evil goes far beyond a comforting presence.

Our experience of evil is always deeply personal and the answer has never been a series of propositions, whether profound or pithy; rather, the answer is a person. This is where Christianity stands alone in providing an altogether surprising solution to evil and suffering by giving us a God who suffers for us and with us in the person of Jesus. For the rest of this book we will explore the Christian doctrines of the incarnation, death and resurrection of Jesus; and the afterlife and its relevance for the problem of human wickedness.

The Incarnation

There is an old story of an elderly man walking down a street when he unwittingly tumbles into a deep, dark hole. A priest strolls by and he cries out, 'Father, Father, help me!' The priest scribbles a prayer and throws it down the pit. Then a doctor passes by and again the man cries out, 'Doc, help me out of this hole!' The Doc responds by writing a prescription and tossing it down into the darkness. Next the man's friend walks by. The man in the hole cries out desperately, 'Joe, Joe, help me out!' Joe stops, looks down at his friend in the hole, and jumps in beside him. The trapped man is bewildered. 'Joe, now we are both trapped in the hole!' Joe turns to his trapped friend and says confidently, 'Don't worry, I've been down here before and I know the way out.'

The above story is a familiar parable about the need we have for other people to enter into our pain and darkness and help us out of the mess.[3] But here is a question: what if all of humanity was trapped in the hole? Where would our help come from then?

If the Bible is true, and our experience isn't misleading us, all of humanity is trapped in the hole of sin, evil and suffering and we can't climb our way out. Given this shared predicament, someone from outside of the sinful hole has to jump into our situation and pull us out. An incarnate God who lived a sinless life is the only one who would be able to do so. If God is good, it seems reasonable that He would choose to do so. As Christians, we believe God has done so in the incarnation of Jesus. Our ultimate justification for this belief is provided by the resurrection of Jesus. The resurrection acts as God's ultimate stamp of approval on the life, ministry and radical claims of Jesus Christ. Unfortunately, we will have to wait until the next chapter to explore this central doctrine of Christianity and its relevance to the problem of evil.

The Trinity

The incarnation brings the reader face-to-face with the Christian doctrine of the Trinity. This doctrine can be stated in this simple manner: there is one God who exists eternally as Father, Son and Holy Spirit, all participating in the great dance of redemption. One divine essence; three distinct persons. The doctrine of the Trinity is not a contradiction, but it is a mystery that goes beyond reason without overthrowing it. Understandably though, many people have difficulty understanding this idea so let us pause for a moment and suggest one possible reason why we stumble over the concept of a Triune God.

A Frolic Through Flat Land

You and I live in four dimensions if you include time.[4] Being four dimensional creatures gives us the ability to move side to side, backward and forward, and up and down. If we were dimensionally deprived by living in one dimension we could only move in a line. If you added a dimension we could go in two directions and draw figures like squares. For the purpose of this analogy let us imagine we lived in a two dimensional land. One day an odd visitor arrived in flatland. He claimed to be from a strange, four dimensional world far beyond the flat hills and the flat sun. He began to speak about cubes. The citizens of flat land scratched their heads in befuddlement. 'What is a cube?' Our four dimensional friend replied, 'A cube is a square made up of six squares.' Blank stares covered every flat face. The philosophers of flat land called a symposium. After much heated discussion the learned in the land concluded such an idea was nonsensical. What, after all, could it mean to say a cube is one square with six squares.

Our brief adventure into flat land has a purpose. We find ourselves in a similar situation when considering the doctrine of the Trinity. Explaining the Trinity to us is like trying to communicate a cube to the hapless folks in flat land. They understand a square. We can comprehend a person. One cube with six squares and one God in three persons, however, are ideas that stretch us beyond the limits of our learning. Therefore, given our intellectual limitations, it seems that the last reasonable act of reason is to humbly confess there are things that go beyond it.[5] The Trinity is one of these 'things', and I doubt it was a doctrine the church would have taken creative liberties with. After all, if I were going to create a religion it would involve a concept of God that people could grasp. Yet the Trinity remains crucial for our understanding of God's nature. To claim that God is love in His very essence is to unwittingly affirm that God is Triune. Love is a relational word, and to claim that God is love, not just in His relation to us, but in His very nature, requires a plurality of persons that the doctrine of the Trinity provides us with.

God With Us

In the incarnation Christians believe the second member of the Trinity, God the Son, took on flesh. The Word, the creative and unifying principle of the world in Greek Philosophy and God's creative agency in Jewish theology, became flesh.[6] The eternal God entered into time; the creator became a creature, and the infinite God became a finite child; from power to poverty, from wealth to weakness, from a throne to a stable. This is the stunning depth to which God willingly condescended to rescue floundering sinners.

Think for a moment of an author writing a novel. Suppose at a certain point of time the author decides to write himself into the story. There he appears strolling down Main Street, whistling merrily to himself, off to see his girl – all in the book of course. He interacts meaningfully with all of the other characters. The author is in the novel and he, as the character, faithfully responds to situations and makes comments that genuinely reflect the author's personality and insight as various circumstances arise within the plot of the story. The author is incarnate in his writing. He is outside of the novel writing it in a manner similar to God the Father, but he is simultaneously really in the book too – like Jesus, the Son.

The representation of the author written into the story line is both fully the author and fully the character in the story in a manner similar to Jesus being both fully God and fully man.[7] This type of analogy (though not perfect if pressed too hard) helps us grasp the concept of the incarnation. God as the author of history wrote Himself into His own story to rescue from certain demise the floundering characters He created.

The Incarnation & Suffering

The above paragraphs were a necessary prelude to discussing how the incarnation of the Son of God speaks powerfully to our suffering. If Jesus is the Son of God, sharing the divine nature of His Father, it means God does not remain aloof and unconcerned about our suffering. Instead, God plunges into the heart of it through the life and death of Jesus. When we suffer evil we realize it is not something we would choose. Yet, God willingly let His Son be crucified by wicked men. The Son of God endured agony on such a scale that it outstrips most of our suffering and this was not divine child abuse either; Jesus didn't have to die - He chose to.[8]

Why?

The answer to that question was mentioned at the end of the last chapter and is the center of the Christian worldview. Love.[9] God is love within His very nature. God loves His Glory and He loves us so He sent His son. Evil in all of its variety may make us question the goodness and love of God. A proper understanding of the incarnation and the crucifixion restores it.[10] The crucifixion might make us doubt the power of God. A proper understanding of the resurrection revives it.

When we meditate on the incarnation, life, death and resurrection of Jesus we still don't receive a full answer as to why we suffer any specific act of evil, but we know what the answer can't be; it can't be that God doesn't love us. He has demonstrated His love once and for all at the cross.[11] You see, central to the Christian message is that God in Jesus gave His life to save us. There is no greater love than when a man lays down his life for a friend.[12] Yet, the Gospel tells us that while we were still enemies of God, Jesus died for our sins.[13]

The more you love someone the more you are willing to suffer on their behalf. Think of what Christ endured on the cross while absorbing the just wrath of God against sin: separation from His heavenly Father, betrayal and abandonment by friends, and physical torment from enemies. Jesus suffered all of this for the Father's glory and for you and me. So, paradoxically, if there was no suffering in our world we would never fully grasp how much God loves us.

When we plant the truth of the Gospel deep in the soil of our hearts it doesn't remove our suffering, but it provides deep-rooted assurance that God is for us not against us, and nothing will separate us from the love of God given to us in Christ Jesus our Lord.[14]

The Savior and the Slum

I once spent several days living on the Downtown Eastside of Vancouver. This six block radius is the poorest in Canada. The amount of human suffering, abuse, hardship and brokenness was overwhelming. It weighed heavily on me as we walked the garbage-strewn streets and explored the neglected neighborhood. How do I, a believer in a perfectly loving and powerful God, cling to that belief in light of the wretchedness that is so pervasive on the Downtown Eastside?

My friend works on the Downtown Eastside in one of the buildings that houses many of the addicts. One man my friend knew struggled mightily with chronic pain combined with an addiction to heroin. But the addict was also an artist because the addict was an image bearer of God. One day he drew for the building's chaplain a poignant picture: A sketch of Jesus on the cross with a heroin needle sticking out of his arm. Jesus offended the religious – that picture birthed out of one addict's pain still does. But if the Christian story is true, Jesus bore our burdens. Jesus became sin for us and suffered with us on the cross. To this addict only a crucified, burden-bearing God makes sense on the Downtown Eastside of Vancouver, and, I would say, in the slums of Calcutta, or in the killing fields of Cambodia.

The incarnation of God in Christ and His willingness to suffer crucifixion goes a long way to addressing the emotional problem of evil and suffering; not by explaining all suffering, but by giving us a profound reason to believe in a good God in spite of it. The emotional resources provided by solidarity in the face of extreme difficulty cannot be underestimated. Facing tragedy with another at your side is a gift of grace that can sustain us through the most grievous of circumstances. God gives us that gift in the

Gospel. God jumps into the pit with us, to carry us through the hardship and to, one day, whisk it all away. This is a God we can still trust in the face of evil and suffering; this is a God who can speak into our pain.

Lessons From The Cross

Not only does the incarnation and crucifixion of Christ assure us God is not unmoved by our agony, the Bible also informs us that God was present in Jesus Christ paying the penalty for our sins on the cross; the righteous for the unrighteous, the holy for the unholy, and the innocent for the guilty.

A Biblical understanding of the crucifixion, therefore, reminds us that evil is not just in our world, but in our own hearts as well. The world is not neatly divided into good people and bad people, because the line of good and evil runs like a unpredictable fault line right through the center of us all. No one has clean hands – not even the 'best', most religious, among us. It was, after all, the moral, religious people of Jesus' day who handed Him over to be killed.

We may be considered good when judged by standards set in place by bad people. But we may also be very bad when judged by the standards set in place by a good God. Think of it this way; my two year old son has been coloring with crayons for months now. In almost every package of crayons there is a white one. In my opinion, white crayons are pointless if you're drawing on white paper – you can't really see any of the marks that you're making. However, when you are scribbling on black paper with a white crayon your drawing stands out starkly on the page. The white appears much brighter when the background is dark. In a similar manner the purity of Jesus shows forth all the more clearly when juxtaposed with our sin. If everyone is rushing to-gether towards the edge of a pit called depravity, it seems as if no one is moving. Righteousness remains relative. Yet, as soon as someone stands apart from the downward spiral of sin, they act as a reference point by which everyone else can see how far they have fallen.

Jesus is that reference point. He is the contrast. He is the white crayon on our black paper. Compared to Him we all fall short. Jesus is loving in situations where we would be tempted to hate, and Jesus is forgiving in circumstances that would call forth our vengeance. Never is this more clear than at the cross. His love is never so bright as when surrounded by the darkness of Gethse-mane's night. When we embrace God's standards of righteous-ness, exemplified in His commands and ultimately in the sinless life of Jesus, we discover our own unrighteousness; our blatant sin that alienates us from a holy, perfect God. This is the bad news.

The cross, when properly understood, forces us to ask some hard questions. For example, we may be concerned about evil in our world, but do we agonize about the evil in our own heart?[15] Or we may stubbornly complain that God hasn't eradicated evil, but are we ready for Him to begin His cleanup operation in our own souls?

Real Talk

You see, the problem of evil begins with an 'I', extends to a 'we', but can't be honestly addressed without taking a hard look at me.

So firstly , the cross reminds us that we must acknowledge that we are perpetrators – we, ourselves, have contributed to the sum total of moral evil in our world. The foremost response we can make to address the problem of evil is to repent of our own part

44

in it. In the words of philosopher Marilyn McAdams, "Continual repentance is not only necessary for the Christian's own reconciliation with Christ, but also the best contribution he can make toward solving the problem of evil."[16] If the theology of the cross reminds us that repentance is a necessary response to the evil in our own hearts, how do we react to evil when we are the victims of it?

No Future Without Forgiveness

When evil events and suffering flood through the front doors of our homes we often ask, 'Why?' 'Why did this happen to us?' We can often answer the 'why' question in the general sense: this is a broken world, we are sinners, Satan and demons are real, and God can send calamity to judge the wickedness of people. However, these are seldom the responses that people are searching for when they agonize over the why of evil and suffering. Rather, it sounds more like, Why this person and not that person? Why us and not them? Why did this happen at this time, in this season? Asking the 'why' question in this manner is a natural part of the processing journey that a person undergoes in light of a tragedy. This exploration should not be short circuited or snowed under by the alien agenda of a well meaning counselor.

But, unfortunately, the specific why is often unanswerable and ultimately unfruitful when there is not an obvious, or direct line, from a person's sin to their personal suffering. Asking why in the above manner places our focus on the past, which we can't change. Often, there is no hope in the past pain remembered, only despair. All hope lies in the future. As a result, replacing the question 'why?' with 'what now?' can point us forward beyond the present pain to a brighter tomorrow. Asking 'what now?' pries open the possibility of joining God in His redemptive purposes that extend even to this unexpected hardship.[17]

The death of Christ not only confronts us with our own sin, it also provides a pattern for us to follow in our own interpersonal relationships and a partial answer to the question, What now?

What Now?

↳ There is hope in this question.

When evil acts are committed against us we have a hard choice to make. We can mirror Christ, or reflect the perpetrator who wounded us. The second option is the most natural response to evil inflicted on us by another. But when we allow another person's evil conduct to determine our own, not only does wickedness not disappear, it also spreads into our own character. To respond to evil with evil allows a cycle of revenge and hostility to be perpetuated that is extremely destructive to human flourishing. Today's victims become tomorrow's perpetrators in the relentless search for restitution of crimes committed and injustices inflicted. Violence begets violence. Hate begets hate. People get hardened in their hostility and healing never arrives.

At the cross Jesus, the Son of God, shows us another way. Instead of responding to hate with hate, Jesus unmasks and conquers hate through love. Jesus confronts evil, not with evil, but with sacrificial love; love that is willing to go to the cross. While Christ is being nailed to Calvary's tree He utters this prayer: 'Father, forgive them they don't know what they are doing.' This is the type of sacrificial love that unleashes hope and healing into a hurting world, that opens up the possibility of reconciliation and joining in God's redemptive purposes. Christians believe that, through the cross, Jesus was confronting evil and offering to embrace repentant evildoers. God, through Christ, was paying the penalty for our sins so that we could be forgiven. Jesus offers this forgiveness to His accusers, and in doing so teaches us how to avoid getting sucked into the cycle of unrelenting violence that has plagued our history. Therefore, part of the answer to the 'what now?' question is forgiveness.

You see, it is true that we are perpetrators – we have all sinned against God and people. But we are also victims. We have all been wounded by sinful people, and for these inherited scars to heal and the cycle of violence to be snapped, we must forgive as Jesus did.

Years ago I attended a criminal court case for the reading of a sentence. A man had been murdered in cold blood. The accused sat in front of the victim's family throughout the long, drawn out hearing. I witnessed the reading of victim impact statements when the bereaved share how the crime has devastated their family.

During the victims' speeches both the mother and the sister choked out these words: 'I can't forgive because forgiving means forgetting.' Their response to the crime was, of course, natural and understandable given the trauma their family had been forced to endure. And who am I to stand in judgment over their personal struggle to forgive? My concern, however, was pastoral and when they spoke those words, tears in their voices, my heart sank. Their family had suffered a great loss, but in refusing to forgive they were unknowingly reading their own sentence; locking themselves in a self-imposed prison of bitterness. I once read, 'Bitterness is like swallowing poison and waiting for the other person to die.' That day in court I wanted to yell, 'You are letting the criminal who stole a brother and a son from you continue to have power and control over you, thereby stealing your own healing.' They were not hurting the perpetrator, they were hindering themselves, and all because of a tragic misunderstanding of what forgiveness really involves.

What is Forgiveness?

If part of the answer to the 'what now?' question in the face of evil involves forgiveness, we need to have a clear understanding of what the concept actually requires. In what follows, I will attempt to clear up a few misconceptions that cling persistently to the word.

Firstly, forgiveness does not mean forgetting. We can forgive without forgetting, but we can't forget without forgiving.[18] Some hurtful actions that we are called to forgive are so traumatic they are almost impossible to forget. Pardoning another person is not about developing amnesia; rather, it is about choosing not to constantly throw back in their face what the person did to you. You release the person from your hostility and free yourself from the burden of carrying it any longer.

Secondly, forgiveness is not stating what the other person did was okay; if that were the case there would be nothing to forgive. Thirdly, forgiveness is not neglecting justice. If a crime is committed, we can both forgive the person and have them arrested at the same time. In a similar manner, God will deal with every sin justly. In the Christian perspective, either a person will repent and receive Christ so that judgment for their sin takes place at the cross, or they will receive eternal judgment from God. Either way, justice will occur in addition to mercy being offered. Lastly, to forego vengeance is terribly difficult, so once we have a clear picture of what forgiveness is (and is not) we also have to be convinced of its benefit in our own lives in regard to emotional healing and personal growth, or Christian discipleship.

The Benefits of Forgiveness

Early on in my ministry I was praying for a young man who was filled with bitterness and finding it very difficult to overcome his anger. As I prayed for him a startlingly picture rushed into my mind. I saw an image of a serpent biting him. The bite left two blood red holes in his pale, white arm. The snake was poisonous and as a result the wounds were festering and the holes refused to heal. Then I witnessed the poison slowly being extracted; the venom was being steadily drawn out and the wound began to disappear. In that moment I realized that in forgiving we're extracting the poison. The wounds won't heal overnight, but as long as the poison remains they will never mend. Forgiveness is the anti-venom that allows our hurts to heal and our hearts to recover when we have been snake-bitten by sin.

Secondly, forgiveness is a part of Christian discipleship and growth in righteousness.[19] The three great Christian virtues are faith, hope and love.[20] Pardoning a person's offense exercises all three of these virtues in a profound and practical way. This specific act of mercy is offered in faith that God will heal and deal; heal you and deal with the perpetrator. Forgiveness also requires a courageous act of hope; hope that a dark yesterday won't cast a long shadow over all of your tomorrows; that, in God's grace, releasing the person from your enmity will somehow dispel the static cling of darkness to your soul, paving the way for a brighter future. Lastly, forgiveness is a strenuous exercise in love; love that pantomimes the God who extends forgiveness to fiends, and extravagant love to His enemies.

Yet, despite the exercise in Christian virtues and the therapeutic benefits mentioned above, forgiveness remains brutally difficult until we transition in our hearts from meditating on what has been done to us, to pondering what Jesus has done for us.

Jesus gives us the ultimate example of forgiveness on the cross. In forgiveness you pay for the other person's offense. You take their evil into yourself, bearing the cost, and then choose to forgive so that you can live a life unencumbered by the burden of bitterness.

Forgiveness involves a death. You let die the desire for revenge, the intense longing to pay the other back, to steal the sword of justice from the hand of God and wield it in His place. Forgiveness often has to be offered before it is felt and the process seems as hard as death, but it is the only death that leads to a possible resurrection of hope and new life. God, in raising Jesus from the dead, places His seal of endorsement on this approach to the problem of personal evil. Suffering love that bears pain before inflicting it is the only approach that God endorses by the power of a resurrection. This is not an approach for the weak; it is for the meek, or those who trust in the resurrecting power of God to right all wrongs and heal all hurts.

Conclusion

The author Dorothy L. Sayers once wrote,

> For whatever reason God chose to make man as he is -
> limited and suffering and subject to sorrows and death
> - God had the honesty and the courage to take his own
> medicine. Whatever game he is playing with his creation,
> he has kept his own rules and played fair. He can exact
> nothing from man that he has not exacted from himself.
> He has himself gone through the whole of human expe-
> rience, from the trivial irritations of family life and the
> cramping restrictions of hard work and lack of money,

to the worst horrors of pain and humiliations, defeat, despair, and death. When he was a man, he played the man. He was born in poverty and died in disgrace and thought it well worthwhile.[21]

Suffering and evil may make us want to spit in the face of God. The crucifixion reminds us that we already did. As Dorothy L. Sayers helpfully points out, 'God had the courage to take his own medicine' – to swallow the bitter pill of sorrow, to traverse the trials of life. As a result, God knows our pain, He knows our sorrows and there is nothing I will endure that He hasn't undergone first.

Someone once stated in reference to Christ on the cross, 'It is hard to stay mad at a God who is in worse shape than you.' Clearly there is therapeutic benefit in taking your anger out at God – I assume God can handle it. The scripture gives you permission. And if the options are between repressing anger leading to depression, expressing anger causing relational breakdown, or releasing anger to God; the third option is the best. There is still, however, some truth to the above quote. It is difficult to stay angry with a God who endured more suffering on our behalf than most of us will ever undergo.

Perhaps, we can even 'forgive' a God like that.[22]

In the end, I may not be able to understand why some evil occurs, but I can trust a crucified God in the midst of it. God has also modeled for us the way forward in our own response to evil. It has often been said that things either get better or bitter. Forgiveness is the antidote to bitter and the path to better, and this should certainly include forgiving ourselves. As C.S. Lewis once wrote, "I think if God forgives us we must forgive ourselves. Otherwise it is almost like setting up ourselves as a higher tribunal than Him."[23]

The path to pardoning our perpetrators may seem like a neglected trail choked with weeds, thorns and thickets, making it difficult for any forward progress to occur. God, however, has been our great trailblazer. In Christ, God has opened up the path to forgiveness and reconciliation, and we are invited to follow faithfully behind Him.

Quote For Reflection

> *It is to be expected that a God who imposes on us much suffering for the sake of great goods will become incarnate, to share hardship which he has imposed on us. This is a reason why a divine intervention should take the form, not just of a miracle, but of God himself living a human life.*[24]

RADICAL EVIL, RADICAL HOPE

A BRIEF REFLECTION

When I flip on the television and hear about a school shooting and children dying, the face of my son rushes uninvited to the forefront of my mind. My insides churn; it seems impossible to fathom the depths of grief that would result from having him wrenched out of my hands by an act of pointless violence.

I didn't realize fatherhood would do this to me. I failed to anticipate that with the birth of my son I would never be able to hear the news in the same way again. Every child, in one sense, becomes your child. It is distressingly easy to see your child's face in their child's fate. News like this sends a shudder through the soul of every parent and forces us to confront our worst fear; the loss of a child.

Anger

Tragic stories like this make me angry too, furious at the evil in our world and humbled by the sinful passions I find in my own heart. Dare I say that the wrath of God against sin doesn't appear like such a barbarous doctrine on these days but, rather, the only legitimate response to unrepentant evil?

I confess that in moments like this I have never understood why people take issue with God's wrath and anger in scripture. After all, isn't it true that when people claim that God shouldn't be mad what they are really insisting is that God shouldn't be good, as if apathy towards evil is a more proper response than anger?

Some theologians have attempted to 'save' God's goodness by denying His wrath when, in fact, they are compromising God's purity and righteousness. This is a sad irony because a God who smiles at sin isn't good, or worthy of worship. I mean, who doesn't get livid at evil actions? Usually, only the evil people doing the evil things. If God is perfect goodness He will get righteously enraged at sin and sinners. God takes sin seriously because He must, not because He doesn't love us.

So when I switch on the news and see unprovoked violence and aggression against the helpless and innocent, and a surge of white hot anger threatens to burst from my chest is it possible, that in that moment, I am more like God rather than less?

I don't know. But it does seem true to say that, "Such anger is the fluid that love bleeds when you cut it."[25]

Either way, I do know that the anger eventually dissipates; I am hollowed out by the hatred of what has occurred, and into that carved out space in my soul rushes a deep, pervasive sadness. And honestly, I just don't want to be here anymore. Please don't misunderstand me. I don't entertain suicidal thoughts.

Here is what I mean: I just get so sick of this world the way it is; broken, crooked, and unjust. I'm tired of knowing that the un-righteousness in our world is a reflection of the sin in my own heart. I am weary of the realization that the seeds of every evil act are buried deep in the soil of my own heart.

Longing

I want all things to be new. Different. Better. Is that a futile hope, a desperate longing? Or is it a subtle reminder that I was made for another world? Perhaps, my feelings aren't playing the role of a false prophet; this world really isn't supposed to be this way.

When these tragedies occur, the non-believer may very well ask, 'How dare we utter the word 'God' in the aftermath of a school shooting?' But it is in the midst of a crushing moment of despair, or grief, where God is most needed – not ideas about God, but the person of God. Apart from God, where is our ultimate hope in the face of evil? If there is no God everything, good or bad, is ultimately meaningless. Atheism removes God and keeps evil creating the problem of ultimate hopelessness.

So where do we turn to find hope? In the Christian worldview we turn to Christ. The Bible tells us that God entered history in Jesus to pay the penalty for our sins on the cross. This truth assures us that God is not unconcerned about evil in our world, or in our hearts. Rather, God loves us enough to enter into our sin-sick world to bring forgiveness, redemption and new life.

When we meditate long enough and hard enough on the person and work of Jesus we still get no satisfying answer as to why some parents didn't get to pick up their children alive and well after the school shooting. But we do begin to see in Jesus' bloodstained brow, and nail-pierced hands, a God who has suffered unprovoked, undeserved violence at the hands of men. We glimpse a God who has suffered loss, who has swallowed the bitter pill of sorrow, a God who has traversed the trials and tribulations of life in a fallen world.

And we're assured that this God loves us. This God is not immune to our pain. And it is this God who is coming again, bringing a new world with Him untainted by the very presence of sin and death. All things will be new. Jesus promised and His words are trustworthy and true. I believe Him and it helps, even when my heart hurts.

New Heaven, New Earth

Today, I will choose to find my hope in the person of Jesus and the promise of heaven. Tomorrow I will have to choose again to believe the promise of God's glorious future.

> *Then I saw a new heavens and a new earth…. And I heard a loud voice from the throne saying, "Look! God's dwelling place is now among the people, and He will dwell with them. They will be His people, and God Himself will be their God. He will wipe every tear from their eyes. There will be no more death or mourning or crying or pain, for the old order of things has passed away." He who is seated on the throne said, "I am making everything new." (Revelation 21:1-5)*

For the believer in Christ, one day there will be no tears, or pain or death. The death and resurrection of Jesus and the presence of the Holy Spirit in our lives are God's guarantee. In fact, the resurrection of Jesus is a pledge to our hearts that the world we all want will eventually arrive. One day, some day, justice will reign, peace will rule, love will win.

But that day is not today.

During one school shooting, a heroic teacher took a group of frightened children and locked them into a small room, bravely barricading the door with a bookshelf. She tenderly held the crying children's faces in her hands and whispered, "The bad guys are here, but the good guys are coming. We have to wait for them."

In the scripture quoted above, God holds our forlorn faces, tired from too many tears, in His proverbial hands and speaks lovingly to us: "The bad guys are here, but the good God is coming. Wait for Him."

Confusion, Clarity and Mourning

As a Christian, I understand why some terrible transgressions occur in our world. We are sinners, this is a fallen world, and Satan and demons are real. But I doubt I'll ever understand, at least on the deepest level, how evil slithered its way into God's glorious creation. And I'll never grasp why this evil happened to this person, at this time, during this season. I'll never know why one lives and another dies.

It is not for us to know. It is better to sit in silence, to pray, to weep, and to mourn with those who mourn.

Join me.[26]

"There will come a time, you'll see, with no more tears, and love will not break your heart but dismiss your fears." – Mumford and Sons

THE BOSTON MARATHON BOMBING

BY STEVE KROEKER[27]

About 3 hours ago, during the 117th running of the Boston Marathon, two bombs exploded near the finish line, killing two people and injuring dozens of others. There are reports of many amputations. The video footage and eyewitness testimony is gut-wrenching. Images of ambulances lined up delivering injured victims to the local hospital. Reporters are calling it, "a deliberate attack on one of the nation's most celebrated sporting events." It's a shocking and horrible event.

How do we respond to such an event?

Weep

The apostle Paul urges us: "Rejoice with those who rejoice, weep with those who weep" (Rom 12:15). Our first response to these events is heartfelt compassion for those who are mourning and hurting. We may have (some) theological answers, but that in no way trumps the call to compassion and love for those who hurt.

I'm always impacted when I think of Jesus when His friend Lazarus died. When He meets Lazarus' sister Mary, it says, "When Jesus saw her weeping, and the Jews who had come with her also weeping, He was deeply moved in His spirit and greatly troubled" (Jn 11.33). He then wept and was moved again when He came to the actual tomb. Even though Jesus knew that He was about to raise Lazarus from the dead, even though He knew the happy ending was right around the corner, He still was deeply impacted by the hurt of his friends and He wept with those who wept.

Pray

We commit to praying for those who are injured. Some are in surgery as we speak. Some have lost limbs and have had their lives changed forever. Even if unhurt, thousands of eyewitnesses have been rocked by experiencing this shocking event. Pray for the emergency and medical workers. Pray for police as they work to protect the public from further attack. Pray as they seek justice and find those responsible. Pray also for the churches in Boston, that they will effectively minister the gospel to their city at this time of need. Pray that the broken-hearted will find hope and healing in Jesus.

Be Reminded of our Brokenness

We live in a beautiful but broken world, a world where great evil is brought upon the innocent. Whether it's a school shooting, or this evil act, we are reminded that this world is broken and corrupted by evil. This is not the way it's supposed to be. The word sin has all but fallen out of use outside the church, and in many cases even inside the church. The word evil is used for only the most extreme of situations. So while our culture struggles with vocabulary to describe these events, we are reminded of the sinful, broken and evil condition of our world. It is beautiful, but broken.

Repent of Our Own Sin

In Luke 13, Jesus responded to two tragic events in His day, one an act of murder, the other a collapsing tower. His response was, "Do you think that they were worse offenders than all the others who lived in Jerusalem? No, I tell you; but unless you repent, you will all likewise perish" (Luke 13:4-5). It seems that people were thinking that these tragic deaths were a result of God's judgment; that they deserved to die this way. That we who survived got what we deserved (life) and they that died got what they deserved (death). The crowd expects Jesus to affirm this. But He doesn't. Jesus corrects this by saying that those who died were no worse than others. We all stand guilty of sin and are in need of repentance.

If we are spared from tragedy and given another day of life it is not because we earned another day, but because of grace. Jesus responds to the tragic death of some by telling those living that they too deserve to die. When I hear of the tragic death of others I quickly am reminded that, because of my own sin, that should have been me. Steve Kroeker should have died today. It is only grace that will see me through to sunset. This tragic and horrible event in Boston needs to drive us to repent of our own sin and cherish God's grace to each of us.

Come, Lord Jesus

When we encounter great evil, we remember that though this world is broken, God has not abandoned it. We don't place hope in education and progress and culture and human spirit to raise us above the evil of our age. We don't place hope in politicians or policies or armies to protect us. We look to our coming King. What we need is the return of the King. Jesus, the rightful ruler and King of this earth will return and establish His kingdom, eradicating sin and evil, defeating death, healing the hurting and restoring all that was broken by sin and death. The problem is sin and the answer is Jesus. The ache in our heart as we watch images of this Boston tragedy leads to a cry of longing, "Come, Lord Jesus.

A DIVINE FOOT IN THE DOOR

CHAPTER 3

In 2009, the Sherlock Holmes' movies hit theatres starring Robert Downey Jr. and Jude Law. The plot of this mystery thriller is captivating, weaving a fascination with the occult and the supernatural together with a hard-nosed logical approach to the evidence surrounding the case Holmes is investigating. As the story unfolds, Sherlock and Watson find themselves dealing with apparent supernatural occurrences, including a resurrection from the dead. One dialogue in particular interests me; it involves a discussion between Watson and Holmes about the villain, Lord Blackwood, who has reportedly conquered the grave.

Watson says to Holmes, "You have to admit Holmes, a supernatural explanation to this case is theoretically possible." Sherlock replies without skipping a beat, "Agreed, but it is a huge mistake to theorize before one has data. Inevitably one begins to twist facts to suit theories instead of theories to suit facts." In another one of Holmes' justly famous quotes he states to Watson, "How often have I said to you that when you have eliminated the impossible, whatever remains, however improbable, must be the truth?"[1]

In my opinion, Watson and Holmes in the above dialogue embody the epitome of rationality. Unlike this dynamic duo, however, many people today unquestioningly embrace hard-nosed skepticism in regard to any alleged supernatural event and, as a result, what is simply improbable (according to some) becomes impossible. Some hesitancy to affirm the miraculous is, of course, warranted. In any alleged miraculous occurrence one should first seek naturalistic explanations to avoid sinking into silly superstition, or a promiscuous use of the term 'miracle'. But what we must resist, I believe, is the modern hegemony of materialism (only natural causes exist) that rules out of court any miraculous occurrences in our world before a thorough investigation is even undertaken.

Of course I realize we are modern people. We have harnessed and tamed much of the natural world through the scientific method. We have littered space with monuments of human ingenuity, including the moon landing of the late sixties. We live in an age of technology and modern medicine so, surely, we can't believe in miracles anymore.

The first Christians, on the other hand, were primitive people, subject to all sorts of silly superstitions. We can now, given our current level of scientific aptitude, affirm confidently that people cannot, to give one pertinent example, rise from the dead. The only credible option is for us moderns to emancipate ourselves from our ancestors' longstanding bondage to mythical models of the universe where 'gods' intervene in the affairs of men, and salvation figures die only to rise again.

Science & Miracles

Our culture has handed many of us an anti-supernatural bias rooted in the pervasive, overarching story sketched briefly above. It is so common to affirm that, through the scientific method, our understanding of the world has progressed to such a degree that it is no longer rational to believe in miracles.

But is this the case? What scientific discovery, after all, has made belief in miracles untenable? Let me ask the reader: Did we need science to inform us that someone walking on water is a surprising feat? Did we require science to explain that the blind normally remain blind; or that the crippled seldom leap to their feet; or that the bodies of the dead have always very predictably stayed dead?

Of course, not! Ancients knew that as well as moderns from frequently repeated experience. In fact, if people didn't naturally sink in water, or dead people weren't always dull participants in a game of hide and seek; we would never affirm water-walking or the resurrection of Jesus as miracles.

Science has, of course, confirmed our oft-repeated experience that people can't naturally come back from the dead. The topic of this chapter, Jesus' resurrection, involves a supernatural event. Science describes and delineates what normally occurs. Science has nothing to say, by its legitimate tools of investigation, as to whether or not God can intervene in our world in a miraculous manner. To say it another way, miracles don't break natural laws, rather, they assume natural laws and add one additional factor, a supernatural agent intervening to accomplish His purposes. Science can tell us that God doesn't normally intervene in this manner, to which the believer would respond, 'Of course, that is why we call these surprising, unusual events a miracle.'

If God doesn't exist, however, then there is no possibility of a miracle, which is, by definition, a supernatural event performed by a divine being. So if the reader of this chapter subscribes to a Godless universe, no amount of evidence will convince him or her that God raised Jesus from the dead. If, on the other hand, it is probable that God exists, regardless of our historical moment or scientific aptitude, we permit the possibility of a miracle such as a resurrection. So let us keep an open mind as we proceed.

Suffering & the Resurrection

In the last chapter we looked at the incarnation of the Son of God and his horrific suffering on the cross. Christians believe that God was, in Christ, reconciling a sinful world to Himself. The profound consolation that this understanding of God gives to the broken and wounded was noted powerfully by the late great theologian John Stott. He wrote that when pondering the sufferings of our world:

> *I could never myself believe in God, if it were not for the cross. The only God I believe in is the one Nietzsche ridiculed as 'God on the cross.' In the real world of pain, how could one worship a God who was immune to it?... He laid aside his immunity to pain. He entered our world of flesh and blood, tears and death. He suffered for us. Our sufferings become more manageable in the light of his. There is still a question mark against human suffering, but over it we boldly stamp another mark, the cross that symbolizes divine suffering. The cross of Christ ... is God's only self-justification in such a world as ours.[2]*

The comfort that arises from the fervent belief that God has shown us His love in Christ, rests on the resurrection of Jesus being a historical event that actually occurred in the course of human history. Apart from this resurrection event, the crucifixion of Christ is part of the problem of evil, not part of God's ultimate solution to it. It is appropriate, therefore, to spend a chapter discussing the subject. At times this chapter may feel like a digression from our topic or a stand alone apologetic for the resurrection, but if you persist to the end it will be worth your while. This is a significant chapter because the Christian answer to the problem of evil, in a large part, centers on the death and bodily resurrection of Christ.

What do we Mean by a Resurrection?

Before we proceed too far in our discussion, however, it is important to define a crucial term - resurrection. By using the word 'resurrection' we are not speaking about a spiritual experience, a subjective vision, a metaphor, or some type of hallucination. In the first century, 'resurrection' meant a transformed physical body untouched by sin, disease and death.[3] For 1st century Jews, the resurrection event was meant to be a communal occurrence, extending to all of humanity, and embracing both the righteous and the unrighteous at the end of human history when all is laid open before God's judgment seat. As prophesied in Daniel chapter 12:2, on this day, "Multitudes who sleep in the dust of the earth will awake: some to everlasting life, others to shame and everlasting contempt."

In 1st century Judaism this is what the word 'resurrection' referred to amongst those who believed in it.[4] The Christian claim, therefore, was unique and unprecedented in that Jesus died, was buried and then appeared to the disciples in a resurrection body in the middle of history. The first Jewish Christians were unanimous in claiming that God raised Jesus of Nazareth from the dead in advance of the general resurrection at the end of human history. This represents, for those familiar with the 1st century world of Judaism, a surprising paradigm shift that is difficult to make sense of apart from the resurrection of Jesus actually occurring.

We will explore below whether or not there are any other compelling reasons to believe that God raised Jesus from the grave, thereby explaining this radical mutation in the world view of 1st century Judaism that gave birth to the rapid growth of Christianity.[5]

I Object!

Before a family sits down to a feast, the table has to be cleared. Unless the clutter that has piled up on the eating surface throughout the day is tidied up, there is no space to arrange the place settings and set the dishes. As a result, the meal can't be enjoyed in the dining room.

In a similar manner, before I outline various historical evidences for the resurrection, I need to sweep away some clutter that may prevent the reader from feasting on the facts surrounding the origin of Easter faith. In the following section we will look at a few brief objections in order to clear the table for the rest of our discussion.

Eyewitness Testimony

According to the New Testament, the Resurrection of Jesus was witnessed by a wide variety of people. A skeptic, however, might say, 'I'm not going to pay attention to this alleged eyewitness testimony because the people listed are biased in favour of Jesus.' The appropriate response is, of course, the eyewitnesses were biased. So what? Couldn't we say back to the skeptic, 'I'm not going to listen to what you just said because you're biased – just in the opposite direction'?

The truth is we all have biases.[6] What follows from that admission? Does that mean we can never report anything accurately, or tell the truth about events? Of course not! In fact, sometimes the exact opposite is true. The most accurate accounts of the holocaust were written by Jewish people – not in spite of their bias, but because of it.[7] When considering the first followers of Jesus, one could imagine the disciples carefully preserving the stories about Jesus because they loved him so much. Moreover, not everyone reported to be eyewitnesses of the resurrection was biased in favour of Jesus. For example, James was a skeptic and the Apostle Paul hated Jesus and Christians. Both Paul and James were originally biased against belief.

In addition, it is unlikely that the first disciples lied about witnessing appearances of Jesus when you stop to consider why normal people lie. Usually the motivation for lying involves getting a reward, or avoiding punishment. As a result, most lying is a selfish enterprise. It would seem obvious that the first disciples of Jesus didn't have the motivation to lie. Christian theologians have tirelessly pointed out that many of the disciples died for their belief that Jesus rose from the dead, and while people die all the time for things they believe to be true (there have been countless martyrs), no one dies for an idea they know to be false. The disciples were in a position to know. The first followers of Jesus didn't die for a theoretical idea like justice and equality for all, but for empirical facts involving an empty tomb and bodily appearances of Christ.

Granted, a resurrection might seem unlikely. But so is a conspiracy where seemingly honest people lie, live difficult lives as a result, and then willingly die horrible deaths for a story they knowingly conjured up. Wouldn't that scenario be incredibly improbable and completely outside of our somewhat limited experience? In fact, I would challenge the skeptic to find another similar example in history where this has happened.[8]

The early church historian Eusebius placed this satirical speech into the mouths of the first disciples:

> *"Let us band together," the speaker proclaims, "to invent all the miracles and resurrection appearances which we never saw and let us carry the sham even to death! Why not die for nothing? Why dislike torture and whipping inflicted for no good reason? Let us go to all nations and overthrow their institutions and denounce their gods! Even if we don't convince anybody, at least we'll have the satisfaction of drawing down on ourselves the punishment for our own deceit."[9]*

Biased or not, Eusebius' fictitious speech clearly shows the ridiculous nature of assuming that the disciples made up the stories about Jesus' resurrection. As Simon Greenleaf, a former Professor of Law at Harvard University writes, "It is impossible that they could have persisted in affirming the truths they narrated had not Jesus actually risen from the dead, and had they not known this fact as certainly as they knew any other fact."[10]

Eyewitness Testimony Varies

When an accident occurs that is witnessed by a large group of people there is often disagreement about the exact details of the crash. People provide conflicting reports about the colour of the cars, the exact time of the crash, or the different extenuating circumstances surrounding the wreck. In light of this inevitable disagreement can we really trust eyewitness testimony?

This objection, based on the supposed unreliability of eyewitness testimony, is misleading. Of course, the witnesses differ about the details. The crucial matter is that they all report that the accident occurred. Discrepancies surrounding incidental details do nothing but prove that the witnesses didn't collude together to fabricate a story. This point is a powerful response to the critic who attempts to cast doubt on the resurrection by seeking to show discrepancies between the various accounts of the event in the Gospels. Not only does our argument developed below not rest on the divine inspiration of the Gospel accounts, but when we consider the eyewitness testimony for the resurrection and the other various strands of circumstantial evidence, all threads converge on the main facts of the resurrection – Jesus died, He was buried and three days later God raised Him from the dead.

Probabilities Not Proofs

The dramatic events surrounding the first Easter occurred close to two thousand years ago. Is it not true that what happened in the distant past is shrouded in the mists of time? Is not our sight obscured by the passage of centuries? How can we accurately construct what took place in 1st century Palestine?

These questions provide a helpful caution for anyone who would attempt a historical reconstruction of any past event. We must not be over-confident when discussing historical happenings, because we are dealing with probabilities not proofs. Historians are attempting to provide a hypothesis that is a reasonably close approximation of the actual event, but all proposals are modifiable by future discoveries or by new ways of exploring and synthesizing old data.

In the end, however, to state that history is unknowable is ultimately self-refuting and unsustainable. For example, even when postmodern writers make the claim that all history is 'dead', they usually assume the validity of their historical sketch of how we arrived at this sorry state.[11]

We can certainly know truth about past events when we are provided with a multitude of reliable sources that are dated close to the events being recorded; especially if the historical sources in question were written by eyewitnesses, or contain the testimony of eyewitnesses. Indeed, the distance separating us from a historical event is irrelevant, if we still possess reliable sources written shortly after the events in question. This also gives us the ability to investigate whether or not a miracle occurred. Historians are not barred by their discipline from adjudicating on a miraculous occurrence even though God is invisible to the normal methods of empirical investigation. Though we can't see the God who performed the miracle, a historian can still explore the facts surrounding an alleged supernatural event.

Since we do possess a multitude of sources for the first Easter event, written close to the event in question, and containing the remembrances of eyewitnesses, we certainly can piece together the events of the first Easter with the normal tools of historical investigation. Many have done so.[12] Even the ardent opponent of miracles appears to unwittingly recognize this fact, made apparent in their stubborn refusal to give up the possibility of disproving a miracle. As Francis J. Beckwith points out: "Disproving the historicity of a miracle is only possible if it is within the bounds of historical endeavor to investigate a miracle."[13]

In the end we will not uncover proofs for the resurrection, for only probabilities await us at the completion of our brief investigation.[14] This is, however, what one would anticipate from a God who does not compel belief, but always provides enough reason to convince the one whose heart is open.

The Pagan Christ

Isn't the story of Jesus' resurrection borrowed from pagan mystery religions? Is the central Christian claim nothing but modified mythology? Despite the popular but exaggerated claims prevalent on the world-wide web, historians have long since refuted the sensational claim that the resurrection of Jesus was stolen from pagan myths like the story of Osiris, Isis, and Horus. A cursory reading of this Egyptian tale will prove to any interested, objective reader that there are no relevant similarities between the resurrection of Christ and this Egyptian story, neither in teaching or literary genre. Osiris wasn't resurrected in the Jewish or Christian sense of the word, he undergoes a crude resuscitation and lives on in the underworld, his shredded body pieced together by his devoted wife Isis.

This example is noteworthy because it is typical of other alleged comparisons between Christianity and the pagan mystery religions (i.e. the cults of Dionysus or Mithras); either the similarities are non-existent, exaggerated, and/or post-date the growth and spread of Christianity (e.g. stories about Apollonius), or they represent similarities that are common to most religions (salvation motifs/promise of immortality etc).[15]

In addition, there is no compelling historical evidence that these pagan stories were known, let alone prevalent, amongst the Jews in 1st century Palestine. On the other hand, there is significant historical data that indicates 1st century Jews were fiercely resistant to pagan ideas, making it unthinkable that the first Jewish disciples of Jesus would construct stories about His resurrection based on unknown pagan mythologies. These provocative but ill-founded assertions represent a school of comparative religion that was, at one time, prevalent in Germany,[16] but is now close to a hundred years out of date. Responsible scholarship has moved on and so should we.[17]

To conclude this section, now that all the clutter has been cleared off the table, we are ready to feast on the facts. Is it true that God raised Jesus from the dead? In what follows we will examine three well-attested historical facts and argue that the resurrection of Jesus is, by a large margin, the best explanation available.

The Eyewitness Testimony

In the Apostle Paul's letter to the confused Corinthian church, he included an early Christian creed regarding the death and resurrection of Jesus. This creed was not written by Paul, he is handing it down to the Corinthian church:

> *3 For what I received I passed on to you as of first importance: that Christ died for our sins according to the Scriptures, 4 that He was buried, that he was raised on the third day according to the Scriptures, 5 and that he appeared to Cephas, and then to the Twelve. 6 After that, he appeared to more than five hundred of the brothers and sisters at the same time, most of whom are still living, though some have fallen asleep. 7 Then He appeared to James, then to all the apostles, 8 and last of all He appeared to me also, as to one abnormally born.*[18]

This early creed states that Jesus appeared to certain eyewitnesses.[19] It is introduced with the traditional rabbinic phrase used to indicate the transmission of received tradition, 'What I received I passed on to you.' Scholars date this creed anywhere from two to five years after Jesus' death.[20] This is too close to the actual events recorded for legend and myth to have overtaken the hard core of historical facts, because friendly and hostile eyewitnesses were still around to refute false stories and testimony.[21] For example, you notice that the apostle Paul writes that 500 people witnessed the resurrection of Jesus and many were still alive at the time of his writing - meaning the skeptic could check the facts behind Paul's claims. Obviously, you don't give people that type of opportunity if you've fabricated a story.

So what we have before us in 1st Corinthians 15 is early eyewitness testimony written down in creedal form close to the actual events it reports that bears witness to the death, burial and resurrection appearances of Jesus.

The above passage states that Jesus Christ died for our sins according to scripture. In the Christian understanding, God is holy so He must punish sin. God is also love so He desires to save sinners. At the cross God's justice is demonstrated in punishing sin and His love is displayed in taking our well-deserved judgment on Himself through His Son. God's love stoops to satisfy the demands of His justice. This is what the first Christians believed and this is the message they fearlessly proclaimed throughout the Roman Empire. Christianity was never good advice; it was always good news about what God had done for people through Jesus.

Now, it is crucial for us to realize that no 1st century Jew would have been predisposed to believe this gospel and the first Christians were 1st century Jews. In 1st century Judaism a crucified Messiah was, by definition, a failed Messiah suffering under God's curse. The Messiah's role was never to die for the sins of God's people. The Jewish notion of the Messiah involved a political, military leader who would defeat the enemies of the Jews, in this case the pagan Romans, not die horrifically at their hands. This is why the first Jewish disciples lost hope for a brief period of time after Jesus died. Given their worldview, they would naturally have thought that Jesus was another failed Messiah - they had backed the wrong horse. In fact, we know as a matter of historical record that in every other 1st century messianic movement when the Romans eventually killed the would-be messiah the followers either went home or found another messiah.[22]

So why didn't the disciples of Jesus follow suit?

Instead, the disciples redefined the Jewish notion of Messiah from a conquering hero to a suffering servant vindicated by God through the resurrection.[23] Though the idea of a suffering servant can be found in Isaiah 53, nothing in Jewish theology anticipated the type of radical reinterpretation of the Messiah made by the 1st Christians, which involved the resurrection of a solitary individual in the middle of history.

All this is to say it is difficult to plausibly imagine a 1st century Jew conceiving, let alone believing for a second, that the death of Jesus somehow paid for our sins, making the temple sacrifices obsolete and much of the sacred law of Moses no longer relevant, if He hadn't risen from the dead.

Given this historical context the first piece of evidence for the resurrection is simply the fact that the first Christians believed the death of Jesus had atoning, saving significance. Jesus didn't die for His sins; He was crucified for ours.

The Empty Tomb

In addition, the 1st Corinthians passage implies an empty tomb by stating that Jesus was buried and raised. A wide range of additional historical data implies the empty tomb of Jesus.[24] Firstly, women were said to discover the empty tomb. This is an unlikely invention of the Gospel writers because the testimony of a woman was looked upon with derision in this culture. Secondly, the tomb was said to belong to Joseph of Arimathea who was a well-known member of the Jewish Sanhedrin, the Jewish ruling council of that day. This is another unlikely creation of the Gospel writers considering how well known Joseph would have been and the fact that there was some animosity between the first Christians and the Sanhedrin who were responsible for handing Jesus over to be crucified. Thirdly, there is an abundance of archeological evidence that the Jews would enshrine and commemorate the tombs of famous martyrs and rabbis. There is no record of this happening at the tomb of Jesus, which is remarkable considering His impact, and strongly suggests His body didn't remain where He was originally buried.[25] Lastly, the Jewish explanation for what happened to the body of Jesus (the disciples stole it) presupposes that the tomb was actually empty. For all these reasons it is logical to assume as a matter of history that the tomb of Jesus was actually found empty.

Transformed Lives

The 1st Corinthians 15 creed also lists a multitude of men and women (the 500), the twelve disciples, James, and the apostle Paul who were eyewitnesses to the resurrection. The transformed lives of the men listed by name in the above passage are beyond dispute historically. It is admitted across the spectrum of scholars that the Apostle Paul was a man who opposed the church ferociously until he was converted by what he claimed was a resurrection appearance of Christ. As a result of this revelation, he lived a life of difficulty, hardship and sacrifice, which ended with a martyr's death. Thomas went from a doubter to a courageous martyr. Peter was transformed from a coward to a fearless preacher and sealed his testimony to Jesus by his blood. James was Jesus' half-brother. The gospels bear witness that James did not believe in Jesus during His ministry, an embarrassing detail that the Gospel writers would not have invented. Yet, in the early history of the church we find James as a leader of the Christians in Jerusalem, worshiping his crucified brother as God. The Jewish historian Josephus tells us that James died a martyr's death for his belief in his brother as the Messiah, God's appointed Saviour.[26] Why did James rapidly transition from a skeptic to a prominent Christian leader, worshiping his brother as the divine Saviour of the world? What transformed Thomas from a doubter into a daring disciple, or Peter from a coward to a courageous contender for Christ? What caused Paul to abandon persecuting the church and embrace planting churches despite overwhelming opposition, hardship and difficulty?

I believe that the best explanation for the theological significance attached to Jesus' death, the empty tomb and the appearances of Jesus, which resulted in the transformed lives of the disciples, is that God raised Jesus from the dead.

Competing Explanations

Other explanations have, of course, been attempted. The hope is always to make historical sense of the transformed lives of the disciples, the birth and explosive growth of the early church and the central claim of Christianity, without resorting to a miracle.

When assessing the strength of various historical hypotheses, pressed into the service of illuminating events in the distant past, scholars use a variety of criteria. These criteria include: explanatory scope (does the hypothesis explain the greatest amount of relevant data?); explanatory power (does the hypothesis do so with the least amount of effort or greatest degree of simplicity?); plausibility (the hypothesis must be implied by a greater amount of accepted truths); less ad hoc (the explanation enlists fewer unsupported assumptions); and illumination (does the proposed explanation illuminate other areas of associated study?).[27]

In his impressive book *The Resurrection of Jesus*, Michael Licona labours for over 600 pages to assess other competing explanations for the bedrock historical facts surrounding the birth of Christianity that are acknowledged by scholars across the board. These facts include: Jesus died by crucifixion, shortly after Jesus' death his disciples had experiences that led them to proclaim that Jesus had been resurrected and appeared to them, and within a few years of Jesus' death, Paul converted after encountering what he believed to be the risen Christ.[28] Licona runs the most significant scholarly proposals through the various historical criteria employed to assess the strength of any given historical reconstruction. The attempts to explain the resurrection by proposing that Jesus didn't really die, or the disciples went to the wrong tomb, or stole the body, are almost universally rejected by all reputable scholars and fail to meet the accepted scholarly criteria listed above. But what follows is one example of a failed hypothesis that is still prevalent today.

Heavenly Hallucination?

Could a hallucination or subjective vision thoroughly explain the appearances of Jesus to the disciples, their transformed lives and the birth of Christianity?[29]

Here are some problems with answering in the affirmative. Hallucinations are individual events not group occurrences (Jesus appeared to 500 people at once); and they seldom (if ever) lead to significant life transformation. In addition, to honestly contend that the disciples had some sort of vision or hallucination does not adequately explain why they used the language of 'resurrection', which meant a transformed physical body in 1st century Judaism. The hallucination hypothesis also lacks plausibility, because it doesn't explain the conversion of the apostle Paul who was not predisposed to have a grief-induced hallucination or vision of Jesus high and exalted at the right hand of God, or the conversion of the skeptic James, Jesus' brother.[30] Moreover, the hallucination theory leaves unexplained the empty tomb of Jesus and is, therefore, lacking explanatory power and scope.[31]

At the end of his thorough study of our topic in this chapter, Dr. Licona's conclusion is that there is no better explanation for the appearances of Jesus, the transformed lives of the disciples, and the birth of the early church than the explanation the church gave from the very beginning – Jesus rose from the dead. He writes:

> *Since the resurrection hypothesis is the best explanation, fulfills all five criteria and outdistances all of its competitors by a significant margin, I contend that we may declare that Jesus' resurrection is 'very certain', a rendering higher on the spectrum of historical certainty than I had expected.[32]*

In addition to the reported appearances of Jesus and the conversion of the Apostle Paul, there are more lines of circumstantial evidence that seem to support the resurrection of Jesus as an actual historic event. For example, as mentioned earlier in this chapter, the women are reported as the first witnesses of the resurrection, which would be an unlikely invention of the gospel authors given the social status of females at that time. In addition, the startling success the preaching of the resurrection achieved in the city of Jerusalem several weeks after Jesus had been publicly crucified just outside the city walls would require, at the very least, an empty tomb. Moreover, the fact that the enemies of Christianity didn't produce the body and the disciples were willing to suffer and die for the claim that Jesus was raised, weighs strongly in favour of the resurrection hypothesis. Also, consider the radical mutation in Jewish understanding from the resurrection as a one time event at the end of history, encompassing all of humanity, to a solitary individual rising in the middle of history, as the first and best of the general resurrection.[33] And let us not forget the abandonment of the temple sacrifices, the Sabbath, and huge chunks of Old Testament law; all religious institutions and rituals treasured by the Jewish people for centuries.[34] All this in light of a crucified man, a failed messiah; or in the Jewish Old Testament understanding, a criminal dying under God's curse on a cross. What cause is big enough to explain all of these dramatic effects?

When weighing all of the uncontroversial historical data together, in addition to admitting the dismal failure of rival hypotheses, it seems warranted to conclude in the words of eminent scholar N.T. Wright:

> *Far and away the best historical explanation is that Jesus of Nazareth, having been thoroughly dead and buried, really was raised to life on the third day with a renewed body (not a mere "resuscitated corpse," as people sometimes dismissively say), a new kind of physical body, which left an empty tomb behind it because it had used up the material of Jesus' original body and which*

possessed new properties[35] that nobody had expected or imagined but that generated significant mutations in the thinking of those who encountered it. If something like this happened, it would perfectly explain why Christianity began and why it took the shape it did.[36]

God's Meddling

The resurrection of Jesus wasn't a brief moment of mischievous meddling on God's part into the affairs of men and women after long eons of self-enamored silence. God does not, as C.S. Lewis so aptly put it,[37] shake miracles into history at random. Rather, the unusual workings of God cluster around climactic moments in redemptive history. The New Testament book of Galatians states that, "But when the set time had fully come, God sent his Son, born of a woman, born under the law, to redeem those under the law, that we might receive adoption to sonship."[38] When Jesus arrived on the scene of human history the Roman 'peace' dominated, one predominant language was spoken across the empire, travel was relatively safe, infrastructure was superb by ancient standards, and the Greek gods had lost much of their oppressive grip on the imagination of the people. After the long spiritual preparation of humanity, on the edge of an exponential growth in human population, when the time had fully come, God sent His son to live, die, and rise.

In the resurrection of Christ God pressed His signet ring into the wax of Jesus' worldview, lifting it out of the realm of religious guesswork and speculation, infusing it with a divine stamp of approval. The resurrection is God signing off on the life, teaching and ministry of Jesus. Not only was a solitary man raised from the grave, an entire worldview was validated; the world picture given expression in the pages of the Old and New Testament.

For the Christian the resurrection shouldn't require a strenuous act of faith to affirm. Given the radical theological claims that Jesus made (veiled hints that He was deity clothed in flesh) and the miracles He performed, acknowledged by both friend and foe alike, one might surmise it quite likely that something unusual would happen to Him once He was put to death. Moreover, it is certainly true that many Christians will believe in the resurrection solely on the basis of their experience of the risen Christ.

To bring us back to the topic of this book, however, evil inflicted, and suffering endured, can be so traumatic that it can, for a time, overshadow and dwarf in significance the comfort granted by the mystical experience of Christ dwelling in our hearts. In these moments of desolation it is heartening to be assured that we have solid reasons to believe that God raised Jesus from the dead; not just as a subjective matter of personal faith, but as an objective matter of historical fact.

The Resurrection and Our Suffering

An author by the name of Nicholas Wolterstorff lost his twenty-five-year old son in a tragic climbing accident. He wrote a book called *A Lament for a Son*, in which, he reflects poignantly on his own grief. He writes about the impact the resurrection of Jesus had during his long season of mourning:

> *To believe in Christ rising from the grave is to accept it as a sign of our own rising from our graves. If for each of us it was our destiny to be obliterated, and for all of us together it was our destiny to fade away without a trace, then not Christ's rising but my dear son's early dying would be the logo of our fate...to believe in Christ's rising and death's dying is also to live with the power and*

the challenge to rise up now from all our dark graves of suffering love...So I shall struggle to live the reality of Christ's rising and death's dying.[39]

Despite all of our earthly suffering, evil, death and injustice do not represent the logo of our fate. The resurrection of Jesus Christ is God's empathic 'yes' to life and love and 'no' to sin and evil. Our destiny is bound up in His – He rose, and through repentance of sin and loving trust in Christ we will rise with Him into a new world free from all that defiles and destroys this one. This is our hope based, not in wishful thinking, but in a concrete historical fact – God raised Jesus from the dead.

Things Unseen

Through the resurrection of Jesus death is defeated. Death will die and life will live forever when connected again to the author of all life. Death remains an enemy, but our future hope, rooted in the resurrection of Christ and the promises of God, has the power to transform our own death on the day of its arrival. Author Mark Buchanan in his book *Things Unseen* tells this story about an older woman in his church named Marlene who had cancer. He writes of Marlene,

> *She was hospitable, an entertainer of angels, a friend to the lonely, the wounded, the perplexed, the sorrowful. The comfort she gave was more than sympathy. She exhorted. She strengthened feeble arms and steadied shaking knees with the Word - and with the example of her own unflinching, matter of fact faith.*
>
> *Marlene, was above all an evangelist. That was the fire in her bones. Every encounter was to her a divine ap-*

pointment, an opportunity to show and, if needed, tell people about the love of God through Christ. God blessed her with extraordinary influence. The throng lining heaven's gateway to thank her will be huge, and larger than anyone on earth knows, for she did her work quietly, without trumpets blaring.

So we asked God to remove the cancer in Marlene. We wanted her to stay with us, among us, to do what few did, to inspire us to do it too. But God said no.

Saintliness is seen as much, maybe more, in our death-style as in our lifestyle. Marlene rose to new greatness in her dying… Her last days were spent in the hospital. Room 318. A strange peace was in the place. Despite the massiveness of her cancer, she was without pain. Her family and some close friends were there, often silent - most words had worn out - though sometimes they sang one of her favorite hymns.

Somewhere in the last days, Marlene's friend Eugene leaned close to her. He took her papery, willowy hand - her cold, cold hand - in his, and held it tight. Too tight. Marlene could barely turn her head, but she looked toward him. And then she spoke in a voice surprising in its clarity and strength. "It's all right Gene. You can let go. Don't you understand? I've lived my entire life for this moment."

Marlene had one regret. It was about her husband, Al. She wasn't sure how he would manage without her. But her vow to him was 'until death doth part us', and death would wait no longer.

Al sat beside her. He held her hand. He didn't notice its coldness. He read her Psalm 121: "I lift my eyes up to the hills - where does my help come from? My help comes from the Lord, the Maker of heaven and earth."

"Marlene," he said, "thank you for forty-five years of marriage." He paused only a moment, and then spoke the words she longed to hear: "Run into the arms of Jesus."

Joy flooded her. In that instant, youth came back to her; a brightness, a freshness, a wonder-struck expectancy that swept away the haggardness and pallor. She sat straight up, jaunty, like a child waking after a good sound sleep. "I've lived my entire life for this moment." And she was gone. Heaven-bent.[40]

This moving true story exemplifies the difference that Jesus and the hope of heaven makes, not only to our lifestyle, but also to our death-style.[41] Christians never say goodbye. Death is not the end. There is a future of glory laid up for those who trust in Christ that dwarfs any sorrows we are asked to bear on earth.

The resurrection of Jesus guarantees it.

An Invitation

Some readers may be standing on the outskirts of the Christian worldview peering in. Parts of this chapter are addressed to you. But still, from your viewpoint the existence of evil seems like an insurmountable objection to belief. Perhaps there has been a personal tragedy in your life that has left you embittered towards the very concept of God. The cross of Christ might not mean much to you. In fact, it may seem like one more example of pointless evil.

I want to invite you to step inside the world of Christian faith where we're all confronted by a God who is not thwarted by our sin and evil, but is redeeming us from it; a God who, unlike us, takes evil in the world as seriously as He takes evil in our own hearts; the God who raised Jesus from the dead testifying that sin, suffering and sorrow don't get the last word; He does.[42]

When we look to the death and resurrection of Jesus, we see the ultimate example of God bringing glory and grace out of seemingly pointless evil. We see a God who is both sovereign and good, confronting our sin and wickedness, and defeating it for His glory and our salvation.

As a result, Christianity provides consolation, hope, and ultimate meaning for the victims of evil and suffering through the saving death of Christ on the cross, His resurrection and the promise of a new world.

Moral depravity and the suffering that results may seem like a thorn in the side of the Christian faith but what other option is there? If we boldly wipe away the existence of God from the horizon of our worldview, the problem of evil doesn't disappear – the only solution does.

I, for one, would rather have God and the problem of evil than the persistent problem of evil with no God.

How about you?

Quotes For Reflection

But please: Don't say it's not really that bad. Because it is. Death is awful, demonic. If you think your task as a comforter is to tell me that really, all things considered, it's not so bad, you do not sit with me in my grief but place yourself off in the distance away from me. Over there, you are of no help. What I need to hear from you is that you recognize how painful it is. I need to hear from you that you are with me in my desperation. To comfort me, you have to come close. Come sit beside me on my mourning bench. - Nicholas Wolterstroff after losing his son in a tragic hiking accident.

Don't minimize grief, maximize Jesus. The Bible tells us not to mourn as those who are bereft of hope, but often we intentionally skirt around the mourning and sprint straight to the hope; skip the death and go right for the resurrection. Jesus didn't. We shouldn't be so anxious to jump over grief, we must journey through it, and move into it trusting that Jesus will meet us there.

THE SECRET SISTERHOOD

BY PASTOR DAVID SMITH[43]

Our Story

Weeping and digging, weeping and digging, I sunk a grave for our unborn child. A day earlier I'd woken to my wife screaming and within five minutes had her in the car on the way to the hospital. There in the hallway, doped up on morphine, she delivered our first child – dead. We asked to keep the body, which seemed like a strange request to the staff. That afternoon, in the most surreal shopping experience of our lives, we looked for a box to put our baby in.

After finding a wooden box at Spencer's, which seemed entirely inappropriate, we left the mall. On the way home we passed the Christian bookstore, normally we'd keep on driving, but that day we didn't. It was just before Easter. Between the racks of cheap 'Christian' tack we found a fitting container for our child, a small porcelain chest with nails on the lid and the words 'He is Risen' on the inside.

Admittedly as we had rushed to the hospital earlier that morning I'd forgotten to grab my Bible. Once we arrived I asked where the chapel was and found one. We'd read 1st and 2nd Samuel together during part of our year of long-distance courting while I finished my education in Scotland. I recalled King David's words in 2nd Samuel 12:23b following the loss of his child, "Can I bring him back again? I shall go to him, but he will not return to me."

C.H. Spurgeon wrote these words, 'Where did David expect to

go? Why, to heaven, surely. Then his child must have been there, for he said, "I shall go to him." I do not hear him say the same of Absalom. He did not stand over his corpse and say, "I shall go to him." He had no hope for that rebellious son. Over this child it was not, "O my son! Would to God I had died for you!" No, he could let this babe go with perfect confidence, for he said, "I shall go to him."

A fellow pastor comforted us with the words, "You're populating heaven," and we rejoiced over the thought that on the day we see Jesus face to face He would also introduce us to our miscarried child - to our miscarried children. God in His sovereignty chose to take others before we celebrated the birth of Baby Boaz.

A Disconnect

Many will find our response to miscarriage mystifying; others could, and have, called it 'overdramatic' – among other things. I expected that kind of response from those who unthinkingly absorb the cultural norms of dehumanizing unborn babies to the extent that we kill tens of thousands of them annually in Canada. I also wouldn't have been surprised to find those outside the Church to fail to understand or show compassion.

What we were unprepared for was the unpreparedness of our Brothers and Sisters in the Church. Some of these people would hold 'radical' anti-abortion positions, and yet upon the loss of a life like those they sought to defend they had no idea how to respond. There's a serious disconnect there that every believer has to come to terms with.

I would hope that most Christians are pro-life because they recognize that all humans are made in the image of God, and not merely for a political cause. That pro-life position should lead us to respect the loss of any life; whether that life is sovereignly ended in the womb, in childhood, in adolescence, in adulthood, or in old age.

Among those that did show genuine care and compassion were a long list of families who had also suffered the loss of miscarriage. One-by-one ladies would confess to my wife, "I also lost a child." And when I say 'confess', that's what it felt like. The words would often be whispered, or mentioned in a conversation off to the side. For many this loss was a secret grief, borne alone.

How sad it is that our counsel to newly-pregnant couples is often to suggest they keep it to themselves, 'in case it doesn't work out.' Is that not a damning exposure of our reluctance to recognize life for what it is and tackle the culture's lie that unborn babies are just 'bags of tissue'? Does it not unveil our squeamishness with the call to actually weep with those who weep, as the Apostle Paul tells us? Are we not ashamed that in the very relationships where men and women should feel most vulnerable we've encouraged a secret sisterhood?

Sharing the Secret

If there's a place on earth that families should be able to openly mourn the loss of their unborn children, it's the local church. If we truly believe that those babies – whether they be first, second, or third trimester – are created in the image of God and a blessing from Him, then we should encourage our families to see that 'baby bump' as such. If that child does then die, it is the duty of the church to grieve with that family and speak true, Gospel-centered hope into their lives.

What that does not look like:

"I knew a lady who had seven miscarriages before she had a 'baby.'"

"You're lucky you weren't far along."

"Be thankful you're young and can try again."

"I had one too, you'll get over it."

Pretending the baby never existed.

Getting frustrated at the grief.

Tritely, unthinkingly, or uncaringly sharing Bible verses.

What that may look like (of course this list is more subjective and requires discernment):

Praying privately for the family.

Weeping with them – for their loss, do not hijack their grief.

Thoughtfully reminding them of God's sovereignty and love.

Providing meals, babysitting, and other forms of practical care.

Helping them pack up the baby's bedroom, pregnancy books, etc.

Removing them from the nursery schedule at church for a season.

Remembering the whole family – each family member may grieve.

Most importantly, it's time that the secret was shared. Miscarriage is a death in the family, both the biological family and church family, that should not be carried alone. I admit that, as a man, my role in sharing the secret is at best limited, and therefore I can only encourage my Sisters to challenge the broken culture around miscarriage, primarily by unashamedly talking about it.

Perhaps you would have the courage to write your own story? Maybe you would finally open up with your friends and family about your grief? It could be as simple as sharing this book, or another article, to do what little you can to make the subject more visible.[44]

Whatever you do, I hope you agree with me that it's time the secret sisterhood is ended and that we develop a more robust and caring culture for those who have suffered such loss. As I close, I'm reminded of the shortest verse in all of Scripture, and Jesus' response to the death of His friend, 'Jesus wept.' - John 11:35.

Continue the conversation at *sufferingwithgod.com.*

THE FINAL CONSOLATION

CHAPTER FOUR

In this final chapter we come at last to the doctrine of heaven, in light of which the Biblical authors claim, "the suffering of this present age are nothing compared to the glory that will be revealed in us."[1] Peggy Noonan, Ronald Reagan's speech writer, penned these insightful words:

> I think we have lost the old knowledge that happiness is overrated - that, in a way, life is overrated. We have lost, somehow, a sense of mystery - about us, our purpose, our meaning, our role. Our ancestors believed in two worlds, and understood this to be the solitary, poor, nasty, brutish and short one. We are the first generation of man that actually expected to find happiness here on earth, and our search for it has caused such unhappiness. The reason: If you do not believe in another, higher world, if you believe only in the flat material world around you, if you believe that this is your only chance at happiness - if that is what you believe, then you are not disappointed when the world does not give you a good measure of its riches, you are despairing.

When we embrace the shrunken-down belief that this world is all there is, was and ever will be, suffering is devastating, crippling - life crushing. We only have one shot at happiness, joy and meaning, and the circumstances of our lives may not coalesce to produce such fruit. The end result is not disappointment, it is devastation - a barren, bleak, wintry existence is all we can 'hope' for.

Or listen to the words of atheist Bertrand Russell who claimed,

> *That Man is the product of causes which had no previ-*
> *sion of the end they were achieving; that his origin, his*
> *growth, his hopes and fears, his loves and his beliefs, are*
> *but the outcome of accidental collocations of atoms; that*
> *no fire, no heroism, no intensity of thought and feeling,*
> *can preserve an individual life beyond the grave; that*
> *all the labours of the ages, all the devotion, all the in-*
> *spiration, all the noonday brightness of human genius,*
> *are destined to extinction in the vast death of the solar*
> *system, and that the whole temple of Man's achievement*
> *must inevitably be buried beneath the debris of a uni-*
> *verse in ruins - all these things, if not quite beyond dis-*
> *pute, are yet so nearly certain, that no philosophy which*
> *rejects them can hope to stand. Only within the scaf-*
> *folding of these truths, only on the firm foundation of*
> *unyielding despair, can the soul's habitation henceforth*
> *be safely built.*[2]

Over and opposed to Russell's bleak, one-world view stands the entire Christian tradition. This world is not all there is, was and ever will be. Rather, it is the rehearsal for something greater, bigger and better than we've ever imagined. This life is the prelude to the main event, the introduction to the forever story, the opening credits of the feature film, in which we have a role, but only because we know the star of the entire show.

This is either true or it is not. If not - break out the cabernet, numb the pain, grab the gusto, and squeeze out as much subjective meaning as can be suckled from the bosom of life. The towering edifice of human achievement will crumble and nothing but nothingness awaits.

If Christianity is true, however, it utterly transforms our perspective on life and suffering. In his celebrated book, *The Problem of Pain*, C.S. Lewis writes:

> *A book on suffering which says nothing of heaven, is leaving out almost the whole of one side of the account. Scripture and tradition habitually put the joys of heaven into the scale against the sufferings of earth, and no solution of the problem of pain which does not do so can be called a Christian one.*[3]

Lewis is right. Heaven matters; it matters so much to our topic that Mother Teresa, a woman acquainted with tremendous human suffering, could state with authority and without apology that, "In light of heaven, the worst suffering on earth, a life full of the most atrocious tortures on earth, will be seen to be no more serious than one night in an inconvenient hotel."

Unfortunately, heaven is a term that is little understood today, even in Christian circles. Many Christians when approaching the doctrine of the afterlife have unwittingly absorbed platonic ideas about heaven that have been confusingly baptized with Christian terminology. Plato, the Greek philosopher, bestowed on his disciples a dualistic understanding of personhood. Dualism, in Plato's understanding, results in the belief that the physical world is bad and the spiritual world is good. In this system of thinking, the body houses the spirit like the prison houses the criminal. Death is seen as the great liberator, the soul's release from its shackles of fleshly existence. Heaven, therefore, becomes a strictly spiritual existence radically differentiated from the physical nature of our earthly existence. This whole approach is as profoundly unfaithful to the scripture as it is unappealing to this author.

Over and opposed to Greek dualism, we are taught by the Biblical doctrines of creation's fundamental goodness and the bodily nature of Jesus' resurrection body that our heavenly existence will in some sense be physical. To use N.T. Wright's memorable phrase, the Bible teaches life after life after death. The scriptures explain that when the believer dies their soul goes to be with the Lord[4] until that day when God renews all things and gives the believer a resurrection body like Jesus'.[5] In the Biblical tradition from beginning to end, God loves matter, after all, He made it. The resurrection tells us He won't destroy our physicality; He will recreate it. We are brought face to face with this stunning reality in the last book of the Bible - The Revelation of St. John.

Revelation

The book of Revelation has been a source of controversy, confusion, and contention throughout church history. Its grotesque imagery conjoined with a startling sagacity and a larger-than-life cacophony of characters makes it a constant source of fascination for scholars and everyday Bible readers. The word 'revelation' means an 'unveiling' or a pulling back of the curtains. In the words of scholar Darrell Johnson[6] the book of Revelation, in part, allows us to see "the present in light of the unseen reality of the future." To say it another way relevant to our topic, Revelation allows us to locate our present suffering in light of God's intended future. In this chapter we will investigate more fully how this picture of the future produces strength and endurance in the present.

When approaching the book of Revelation it is important to remind oneself that the Bible should not be read literally but literarily - that is according to its genre. The genre of Revelation is apocalyptic. Apocalyptic literature is visionary, it is highly symbolic, (including the use of numbers as symbols) and is often filled with a cosmic battle between God (or good) and evil. Revelation contains all of these elements to greater and lesser degrees.

Though Revelation is highly symbolic, even symbolism contains literal truth. For example, we will encounter in Revelation 21 a description of the new heavens and the new earth where we are told "there was no longer any sea."[7] The sea in the ancient world (and in the Psalms) often represented the forces of chaos and evil. The symbol of the sea does, however, express a literal truth. There will be no more chaos and destruction in God's renewed creation.

Revelation 21, 22

Contrary to much popular but misguided teaching on Revelation, I believe strongly that much of the book was meant for John's day and is directly relevant for his original audience struggling under the oppressive persecution of the Roman Empire.[8] But it is clear to all readers of Revelation that chapters 20 to 22 speak of events that have not yet taken place. In these final chapters of the book (and the Bible) we witness the final marriage of heaven and earth. The Bible begins with a wedding and it ends with a wedding; a celebration, a joyous occasion where all traces of boredom are banished. And in this refurbished cosmos some activities that are often associated with church will certainly be taking place: worshipping Jesus, singing songs of praise, relationship with other believers, and much more will find their way into God's renewed creation.

There will be, however, far more taking place in the presence of God. For example, in Revelation 20 we see that the wealth of the nations is brought into the new Jerusalem. Among other things, this means that cultural activity will take place in the new heaven and the new earth. The creation mandate given to humanity in Genesis chapter 1 will not be revoked, it will be redeemed. We will still create; exploration, art, music, engineering and many other types of redeemed cultural creativity will find their way into the new world. All that is good, all that is glorious, all that is beautiful and true will be made new in our forever home.[9]

Evil and Suffering

What about the existence of evil and suffering? In Revelation chapter 21 God makes this promise to His people:

> *Then I saw a new heavens and a new earth for the first heaven and the first earth had passed away, and there was no longer any sea…And I heard a loud voice from the throne saying, "Look! God's dwelling place is now among the people, and He will dwell with them. They will be His people, and God Himself will be their God. He will wipe every tear from their eyes. There will be no more death or mourning or crying or pain, for the old order of things has passed away." He who is seated on the throne said, "I am making everything new." (Revelation 21:1-5)*

This is the Biblical picture of our future hope. Here we witness the great cosmic renovation we mentioned earlier in this chapter. As it has often been stated, you notice that God doesn't claim 'I am making all new things,' rather He states, 'I am making all things new.'[10] Think of it this way; one of my friends invests in old, run down properties. He will buy a place, fix it up and then sell it for profit. He has entered some homes where paint is peeling from the walls, fungus is growing on and under the carpet, the plumbing is shot and the rickety roof leaks at even the promise of rain. The structure is often good, however, the insides simply need to be gutted and refurbished. The worse-for-wear home represents the current state of our world filled with sin, suffering and sorrow. What we are witnessing in Revelation 21 is not a complete demolition but a comprehensive, all inclusive renovation.

It is striking when we realize what is missing from this new creation. There is no longer any sea. As mentioned previously, the sea often represented the forces of evil and chaos – they are no more, banished forever from the presence of God and His people. In addition, there is no temple in this new creation. Throughout the Old Testament the temple was the place where heaven and earth intersected, the space where God's presence uniquely dwelt. There is no more temple because God's people are the temple and His presence floods the new creation.

We also find that the New Jerusalem, the city of God, is in the shape of a cube. Those readers who are familiar with the Old Testament will know that in the temple the Holy of Holies, the most sacred place, was shaped in a cube. In the new creation the entire city becomes the Holy of Holies. In the present, the believer often clings to the goodness of God in the midst of evil because he or she has tasted the sweetness of God's presence in the midst of His people. But, in the new creation, God's presence will not be a trickle, it will not be a flood; it will be an overwhelming ocean that we will sink into. Our long exile from His presence will be forever over. We will be home. The most glorious moments of God's nearness are only dim premonitions of what is in store for us. We will be vessels tossed into the infinite ocean of God's love, filled to over-flowing. There will be no lack, no loneliness, no seething sorrow, because the light of God's presence will chase away all our shadows. God's presence won't be a lifeline then - it will simply be Life.

Most striking for our purposes, however, is the absence of tears, pain and death. All of these elements shape and define our human experience in countless ways. It has been noted by authors like the late C.S. Lewis that even love in a fallen world requires suffering because love undergoes and endures countless partings. But Revelation 21 puts a ticking time bomb next to all of our tears. Love will no longer suffer loss.

The wedding banquet will have come at last. A marriage freely chosen will be forever consummated. Joy will overflow, celebration will ensue – all will be well. This is the Christian picture of heaven.

In Light of Heaven

Philosopher of Religion, Marilyn McCord Adams, argues convincingly in her book *Horrendous Evils and the Goodness of God*, however, that all evil can be justified if God provides the sufferer with an incommensurable good in the afterlife that outweighs the suffering in our present world.[11] Christianity proclaims that this is a real option for all children and those adults who choose it. The joys of heaven painted in the preceding paragraphs are said to outweigh all the trials of earth, according to the New Testament scriptures. St. Paul, a man deeply acquainted with suffering, wrote, "I consider that our present sufferings are not worth comparing with the glory that will be revealed in us."[12]

To show how this could work, perhaps a thought experiment

will help. Imagine you experienced the most horrendous day but were given a guarantee that the next 364 days would be exceedingly joyous, filled to overflowing with laughter, contentment, health and deep fulfillment. Would that knowledge (although not taking away the difficultly of the current day, or minimizing any tragedy endured) allow you to persevere with hope and strength, providing incredible resources to cope with your present difficulties? I think the honest answer must be yes. Heaven functions in a similar manner for the believer. We can always travel through dark valleys with hope provided by the knowledge that this life is the worst it can ever get and the best is yet to come.

Heaven as the Postscript?

The problem for many Christians, however, is that we live as though heaven is the P.S. and this life is the main event.[13] We have exactly reversed the position of the New Testament writers, for whom heaven was the main attraction.

Imagine you go to a movie theatre with a friend. The lights dim, voices are hushed and eyes turn expectantly towards the flickering screen. When the advertisements begin your friend leans forward; eyes glued to the images flashing across the screen.

Twenty minutes later the movie begins and your friend leans back into his seat, pulls out his cell phone and proceeds to send text messages throughout the entire course of the movie only occasionally glancing up at the film. After the main feature you berate him, "Why did you watch the previews and basically ignore the movie?" In reply he states, "What I really love are the commercials, but I'm not as interested in the main feature. I like being in the theater so I have the option to watch if I want, but

I'm not too enamored with the actual show." You would think your friend was silly to neglect the main feature in lieu of the advertisements, paying a hefty amount to watch the commercials which only last a few minutes.

Christians (and non-Christians) do a similar thing, however, when we pursue the things of this earth destined to perish, and neglect the unbridled promises of Christ in regard to our eternal destiny. To continually misdirect our affections solely towards earthly affairs makes our experience of suffering on earth far more devastating and joy crippling. Contrast heaven as the post-script to life with the view expressed in the C.S. Lewis children's epic *The Last Battle*. The scene depicted below describes the main characters' entrance into God's heaven. Lewis writes:

> *The things that began to happen after that [death] were so great and beautiful that I cannot write them. And for us this is the end of all stories, and we can most truly say that they all lived happily ever after. But for them it was only the beginning of the real story. All their life in this world and all their adventures...had only been the cover and the title page: now at last they were beginning Chapter One of the Great Story which no one on earth has read: which goes on forever: in which every chapter is better than the one before.*[14]

Similarly to this, heaven is not the postscript. Heaven is the consummation of the grand story into which God invites us; a journey that begins now and continues throughout eternity; a true story that is made possible through Jesus' death for sins and His resurrection from the dead. God invites us to participate in His great story, to be a principal actor, to play a meaningful part, to join joyfully with God in the restoration of all things that begins now and is consummated in heaven.

But heaven, of course, is a world of love. And love can't be forced, it must be offered and accepted. The free nature of love, however, hints at the dark possibility that this love could be forever rejected.

Jay: *Let me let you in on a little secret. There is no such thing as hell.*

Manny: *So everyone gets into heaven?*

Jay: *Yes, everyone gets into heaven.*

Manny: *What about the bad people?*

Jay: *The bad people get placed in a special room.*

Manny: *What if they get out?*

Jay: *They can't. The special room is surrounded by great walls of flame.*[15]

(Modern Family: Season Two – Episode Three)

The Dark Side: *A Dialogue*

Brandon - I agree that heaven is a beautiful idea. If it were real it would go a long way in addressing the problem of evil. You are, however, conveniently ignoring the darker side of the Biblical account. What about the doctrine of hell? The suffering of the wicked never ends. In fact, doesn't Revelation say that the smoke of their torment endures forever and ever?

Chris - The book of Revelation does say that.

Brandon - Do you believe it?

Chris - Yes, but it is worth pointing out that the language is symbolic and metaphorical. Jesus uses both fire and darkness to refer to hell. Hell can't literally be a place filled with flames and simultaneously covered by darkness. Jesus is speaking metaphorically.

Brandon - I've heard preachers state emphatically that the language about hell symbolizes an even worse reality.

Chris - Well, that is usually how symbolism works, but I bring up the symbolic nature of the language to diffuse the common anti-hell rhetoric that refers to it as a torture chamber where God is compared to an evil parent holding a rebellious child's hand over the white hot flames, rejoicing in the smell of burning flesh. At this point the atheist and I have something in common - we both don't believe in this type of God. The difference is my disbelief is grounded in the character of God and the teachings of Jesus.

Brandon - Okay. But hell still sounds like a horrible idea. This may be the key issue that is keeping me from becoming a Christian. How do you reconcile that horrible idea with an all-good, all-powerful God? How can a loving God send people to hell?

Chris - I don't like hell either, but that admission says more about my psychology than the truth of the matter. I will leave, for a moment, whether or not God 'sends' people to hell and for the sake of argument assume He does. I would respond to your question by asking, how can God not? Consider this illustration: My wife and I own a townhouse. We have two young children. We have set up our house in such a way that our children can be holy, happy and safe. Other children are welcome to come over and play with our toys and hangout with our children because I truly love the neighborhood children. There is not a child that I hate. I only ask one thing: they have to obey my rules while they are at my house. The rules aren't meant to be oppressive; they are meant to contribute to the joy of the children.

Now imagine the neighborhood children came over and smacked my son, threw sand in my baby girl's eyes, or gave me the middle finger. I would say to those children, you are welcome at my house provided you will play by my rules. But if you are going to hurt my children and disrespect my rules and my authority, I will have to remove you, build a fence, and get a guard dog to keep you out.

Those deviant children might stand out on the street and complain. "Hey, why won't you let us into your house? You're a pastor. We thought you were supposed to be full of love." But my children would be on the inside of the fence saying, "And he is loving. He loves us enough to protect us from you."[16]

In a similar manner God is our Father. Heaven is His house. All are welcome provided they respect the Father, play by His rules and know His Son. But if they want to reject His will, give Him the finger and hurt His children, He has no choice but to remove them from His presence, and that is hell - a dimension of reality where those go who don't want to submit to God's authority.

Imagine if God let unrepentant sinners into heaven. Heaven would quickly degenerate into hell. Can you imagine if the children of God were still getting used, abused and victimized in heaven? We would go to God and say, "What is the deal?" And if God said, "Well, I'm a loving God," we would respond, "It sure doesn't look like it."

Brandon - Interesting analogy; I thought you were going to go straight to free will again.

Chris - Well, I think free will comes into it. If people were forced into heaven against their will, heaven might be experienced as 'hellish' for that person. Heaven is a world of love; love can't be forced, it must be chosen. My friend Jon[17] likes to say that if Jesus is the only show playing at the movie theater and you don't love Jesus, you will go bowling instead. Hell is bowling.

Brandon – It seems trite to compare hell to bowling but I understand your point. I once read a popular Christian author on this subject and he wrote this:

> I would pay any price to be able to truthfully say "All will be saved." But my reason retorts, 'Without their will, or with it?" If I say "Without their will" I at once perceive a contradiction; how can the supreme voluntary act of self-surrender be involuntary? If I say "With their will," my reason replies, "How if they will not give in?"[18]

So the idea is that God gives some people what they want and often that is a life without God. In this case hell would be the result of God's love (His justice after all is just one expression of His love) and our free will.

Chris - That is definitely one way to look at it. Or think about it like this: Imagine your friend has an awful toothache and they are constantly complaining to you about the pain. You suggest that they go and visit a dentist, but they refuse to take your advice. After a while your initial sympathy for your friend's plight begins to wane. After all, treatment is available but your friend refuses to seek out the skilled hands of the dentist. Your companion continues in their self-imposed suffering. In this situation you certainly don't blame the dentist for your friend's sad situation.

In a similar way, sin is like a proverbial toothache that is destined to be plucked out in God's dentist chair. Yet we must submit ourselves to the remedial treatment; we have to place ourselves in the care of the good dentist. There will be pain, no doubt. Dying to self is never a pain-free process for those of us who have been obsessed with self for so much of our lives; it is, however, a hurt that heals.

In the end, hell would only be for those who refuse the necessary surgery. Hell is like a toothache that goes on for eternity. We can't justly blame its existence on the dentist who, upon our simple request, has always been willing and able to swoop in to accomplish the required surgery on our behalf. I guess, in this sense, God doesn't create hell. We do by refusing to submit our wills to His.

Brandon - Hmm. Okay I guess, but if hell wasn't a part of God's original creation and it is something we create by the abuse of our free will or by refusing the necessary surgery in your words, what happens to the mentally handicapped, or children who have no real chance to choose or reject God?

Chris - I'm not really sure but based on the fact that Jesus uses children universally to symbolize life in the kingdom of God, and based on the fact that infants and mentally disabled people are not capable of responding to God's general or specific revelation, I would contend that they are welcomed into heaven by God's grace. There are a few scriptures that Christians quote to support this perspective, but I can't get into it here.

Brandon - Okay, but for those who aren't saved, wouldn't it make more sense for God to simply snuff them out of existence? In fact, I once heard a pastor say that this is actually what the Bible teaches.

Chris - I've heard that too. I don't think it's right though.

Brandon - Why not? There are some notable theologians who teach conditional immortality. The dead are judged, punished in accordance with their sin and then snuffed out of existence. God alone possesses immortality. This immortality can be given to humans conditioned upon their response to God's loving invitation, but those who reject God's gift are annihilated. Isn't the wage-for-sin death? Both body and soul die - they are annihilated. The use of the word 'eternal' indicates the permanent result of the judgment not the endless duration of it. Haven't you read those verses in the Bible that mention the unbeliever being destroyed? Even the imagery of fire can convey the idea of disintegration and destruction. I've done my research. Jesus says both body and soul can be destroyed in hell (Matthew 10:28. Also see 2nd Peter 2:6; Jude 1:7; Ps. 37:2,9,10; Mal. 4:1-3; Revelation 20:14,15)

Chris - Right, well, it is not like this position rejects Biblical authority per se. However, the position has not caught on in conservative Christian circles because it doesn't appear feasible in light of texts that indicate eternal bliss for the believer alongside eternal loss for the unbeliever. For example, in Matthew 25:46 Jesus states, "Then they will go away to eternal punishment, but the righteous to eternal life." According to Jesus in this passage, the after life is conscious for the believer, so why would we assume it is unconscious for the non-believer? That is certainly not the most natural way to read the text! (Also, see Daniel 12:12) Moreover, Revelation 14:10,11 implies the same idea even more clearly. Not only that, Jesus explains in his teachings that there will be different degrees of punishment in the afterlife, but this position seems to relegate all of those outside of a saving relationship with Christ to the same punishment. (Matthew 11:20-24, Luke 12:47,48) I sympathize with this perspective, but I am skeptical about its faithfulness to the scriptures I've mentioned. When I read these theologians it often feels like they are trying to explain away the clear teaching of certain scriptures, rather than faithfully understand and apply what the texts originally meant.[19]

Brandon - I'm not convinced, but let's say you are right. Here is another question: if, according to your understanding of Jesus' teaching, God doesn't snuff people out of existence, here is another significant problem. According to you (and the Bible) hell is eternal. How is it just for God to punish finite sins for an eternal duration? The concept of an everlasting hell seems to compromise our understanding of justice, thereby casting doubt on the goodness of God.

Chris - But wait a minute, the length of time it takes to commit a crime has no bearing on the duration of the punishment.[20] For example, a person could plan a robbery for three years, get caught and go to prison for five years. Whereas another person could commit a murder in ten seconds and spend their entire life in prison. The length of time taken to commit the crime is irrelevant to the length of the sentence. What matters is the magnitude of the crime. Our sin is an offense to the infinite worth of God - a willful assault on His incomparable value. A sin against an eternal God is an eternal sin that should lead to eternal separation from Him. That's not only fair, it is necessary.

This question also makes some unwarranted assumptions. It seems to imply that a person sins once and then is banished from the presence of God for eternity. A more likely scenario is a rebellious, obstinate sinner who is unwilling to bow the knee to Christ throughout all of eternity. The sinner's situation, therefore, is more like the criminal who is sentenced for a crime and then continues to break the law from inside of the prison, thereby, extending his sentence indefinitely. I don't know if this is the best way to think about it, but this quote has helped me in the past and succinctly captures some of what I've been saying:

> Hell's punishment fits sin's crime because sin is divorce from God. The punishment fits the crime because the punishment is the crime. Saying no to God means no God. The point is really very simple. Those who object to hell's overseverity do not see what sin really is.[21]

Brandon - What about those who don't hear the Gospel and get no chance to choose or reject Christ?

Chris - Well, again I am not entirely sure how it all works, but based on the character of God and the witness of scripture, particularly in the book of Acts, I believe no one will be able to say, "I would have believed if God had just given me the opportunity." If someone's heart is open, God will send that person the gospel through a missionary, a dream or in some other miraculous way. Therefore, an accident of geography or time does not condemn a person. Direct and indirect scriptural support for this idea is enormous. See Hebrews 11:6, 1st Chronicles 28:9, 2nd Chronicles 15:2, Psalm 9:10, Psalm 146:17, Proverbs 8:17, Jeremiah

29:13, Acts 8:30-31, and Acts 10:22-39. Other Christians think that God will judge people based on how they would have responded if they had heard the Gospel. Or maybe God graciously elects some to salvation while allowing others to remain locked in their sinful desires. Christians have held to all of the above perspectives.

Brandon - So where do you land?

Chris - You can investigate those debates for yourself, but in the end when it comes to this question (and really all of the above questions on this topic), I am certain that God is fully revealed in Jesus Christ. The God who is revealed in Jesus is good and just, so whatever God does is right. No one will be able to say to God, "This isn't fair." In fact, fair is getting what we deserve; in Christianity we call that hell. Grace is getting what you don't deserve; in Christianity we call that everything outside of hell, including heaven. I would renounce your right to fairness in this particular instance. Fairness died on the cross with Jesus. But don't worry; grace is much better!

The greatest scandal to 'fairness' in our God-saturated world is a dimension of reality called heaven populated with people like you and me. Just think: treasonous usurpers treated as sons, fearless deifiers adopted as daughters; such is grace - it makes princes out of paupers and princesses out of prostitutes. Anyway, not to beat an already bleeding horse, but God is perfect goodness and justice. I can trust He will do what's right by all people.

Brandon - Yes, but look, does believing in hell require me to tell my good friend, whose lovely, unbelieving mom recently passed away from cancer, that she is now burning in hell? What if he asks me about her eternal destiny? What would I say?

Chris - Oh man, that is brutal. To answer your question, no, I don't think you should condemn his mother to hell. I would say to your friend that his mother sounds like a lovely woman who should be honored for the kind things she did throughout her life. Then I would admit the truth that I have no idea what type of business his mother did with God before she passed away. All we are saying is that Jesus is the way to God and apart from Him there is no eternal life.[22] I realize that we all have ancestors or family members we love that appear to have died outside of a saving relationship with Jesus. This is difficult, but we must remember that we don't always know where a person is in their relationship to God during the last moments of their life. We don't get to make the final call on who is in and who is out. But choosing to stubbornly remain outside of God's saving grace because of our concern for the unknown fate of others is certainly not reasonable. Meanwhile we must obey Him by carrying out the Great Commission and the Great Commandment. We can leave the rest in His hands.

In the end, whether a person is an annihilationist or embraces the traditional, and, I think, more Biblically faithful understanding of perdition, hell provides no rational obstacle to our understanding of God as all-good and all-powerful. In fact, God's goodness and justice require a hell for all unaddressed evil that takes place in our world. As for the emotional problem that hell tends to create, I'll end this section with some frequently quoted words on this topic:

In the long run the answer to all those who object to the doctrine of hell is itself a question: "What are you asking God to do?" To wipe out past sins and, at all costs, to give them a fresh start, smoothing every difficulty and offering every miraculous help? But he has done so, on Calvary. To forgive them? They will not be forgiven. To leave them alone? Alas, I am afraid that is what He does.[23]

To Good To Be True

In this chapter we have been discussing the afterlife. For some, however, the Bible's picture of a new heaven and a new earth strains all credulity. The Christian's belief in God's great cosmic renovation is made more plausible, however, by several factors discussed elsewhere in this book including: Firstly, God created the heavens and the earth (this means God could certainly recreate them). Secondly, God raised Jesus Christ from the dead as the first great act of recreation. Thirdly, God has planted a desire deep in our hearts for heaven. C.S. Lewis argued famously that people don't have desires unless there are corresponding objects that exist to satisfy those desires. We get hungry, there is such a thing as food. We have sexual desires and there is such a thing as sex. Lewis then springs his rhetorical trap on the unsuspecting reader when he writes that "If within in our hearts we find the desire for something that nothing in this world can satisfy, the best explanation is that we were made for another world."[24] Most of this chapter has been designed to help the reader find within themselves a deeper desire that cannot be satisfied by any earthly thing – suffering in fact, is often pressed into the service of awakening us to this (often) buried desire for a better country – a heavenly one. (If all were perfect we might never seek it. We certainly wouldn't desire it as we should.) Taken together, these streams of evidence flow into a rushing river that sweeps us up into the redemptive purposes, plans and promises of our Creator, in addition to providing us with rational justification for our hope in God's heaven.

Aim at Heaven, Get Earth Thrown In

Throughout this chapter we have been discussing the topic of evil and suffering and the new heavens and the new earth, but in doing so there is a danger that we would become so heavenly minded that we would neglect the abundance of earthly good that God provides for us to enjoy. The hope of heaven should both dwarf our suffering and deepen the pleasures and beauties of earth when we receive them as rumors of heaven, whispers of what is in store for the righteous redeemed, sunlight that is to be traced with gladness back to its source in God Himself.[25] Philosopher William Lane Craig was surely correct when he wrote:

> When I first became a Christian, it struck me that in order to obtain eternal life in heaven, it would be worth it if God asked us to undergo an earthly life of the most extreme asceticism, suffering and self-denial, but that God in His graciousness doesn't even ask us to do that; instead, He fills our lives with peace, joy, love, meaning and purpose.[26]

If heaven is real, enduring hell on earth would be worth it to obtain eternal bliss. But, by God's grace, we never fully endure hell on earth. Most of our lives are still interspersed with an abundance of beautiful, soul satisfying moments that make existence persistently preferable to nonexistence.

One Final Dialogue

Sally - Do you think it's good that God created the earth considering the amount of evil in our world?[27]

Chris - I would have to say 'yes'. God is good and only does that which is good. But I still don't understand why so much evil takes place.

Sally - Me neither. But I still think there must be more good than evil or more people would commit suicide and fewer people would have children. I often wonder if our reasons for having children are similar to God's reasons for creating?

Chris - I don't know the answer to that but I do think we often fail to appreciate the many good things that God sprinkles into our lives.

Sally - Like what?

Chris - Simple things. The warmth of the sun on our faces. The smell of barbecues in the summer. The dawning of spring after a bleak winter. A runner's high. A warm shower on a cold morning. A lager and laughter with friends. A lover's kiss. A beautiful sunset. A listening ear. Solidarity in the face of suffering, or spontaneous laughter in solemn moments.

Sally - Yes! I love to laugh. Over the top, making breathing difficult, bringing tears to the eyes, type of laughter. The best of these moments aren't relegated only to the privileged either. Or about a great book and a warm cup of coffee? Or romantic love. Music. Intellectual insight; or the pleasure of comprehension. The cooling of romantic love replaced by deep affection, intimacy and oneness. A marriage with lots of miles.

Chris - Don't forget sex.

Sally - In marriage?

Chris - Yes. Bees belong in the beehive not buzzing unchecked throughout your house.

Sally - Ha, I get the metaphor.

Chris - Well, life is a gift containing all of these treasures. It makes me want to pause and ask my friend the atheist: Don't you feel deep down somewhere that life is a gift? A frail, fragile, mysterious gift? Perhaps, it's not the accidental collision of atoms, a cosmic coincidence, a meaningless meandering through time and space. What if that intuitive hunch isn't just a naked sentiment arising in a moment of emotional vulnerability? What if life feels like a gift because there is a Giver?

Sally - Gratitude would be appropriate.

Chris - You see, if the sorrows of this world were transfigured into tears we wouldn't drown in the flood. God has kindly tossed us many life-lines to keep our heads above the water. We grab them every time we celebrate all of His gifts as evidence of His unmerited common grace.

Sally - Right, I guess if the only data I had was of all the evil in the world it would be pretty hard to believe in God.

Chris - But evil is not all the data you have, is it?

Sally - No, like we've been talking about. Not only are there many good arguments for God's existence, there is the person of Jesus, my experience of God's presence, and the pleasures, joys and beautiful moments I have been grateful to experience.

Chris - Exactly, and all of these various things make the existence of God probable even in the face of evil. To come back to your earlier question about having children – I believe that love creates. Always. Until we decide to no longer bring children into this world it may be unfair to impugn God for suffering and evil in this one?

Sally - Huh, why?

Chris - Well, we all have children knowing that they will suffer to some degree physically and emotionally, all the while wishing it weren't so. Some suffering we impose because we know it is for their long term benefit - six months' shots come unwittingly to mind (do you ever wonder if we're all six-months-old spiritually?) - showing that even good and loving parents allow their children to suffer, though never abandon them in the midst of it. Yet, as parents we still choose to participate in God's creative activity. We deem it well worth our while so that our children may share in our love. When my wife and I had our first child, the birth of our son was our emphatic 'yes' to life - our life-long testimony that we believe the good outweighs the bad; the beauty outweighs the brokenness; the grace outweighs the sin; and the salvation outweighs the sorrow.

We're drawing near the end of our discussion and I don't want to lapse into sentimentality or end with a hallmark moment. Evil exists. Suffering never feels serendipitous. This may not seem like the best possible world but, perhaps, it is the way to the best possible world. One where choice is real, where love is meaningful, where salvation is available, and worship and virtue are made possible. These great goods outweigh the banality of evil in the end and if these great goods could only be achieved by the amount of bad we witness in our world, who am I to disagree?

I'm unsure how much God's reasons for creating all things coincide with our reasons for having children. Perhaps they are very different, but the Bible says God created for His glory. The most loving, self-giving thing a being of pure love and goodness could do is create other persons to enjoy Him. God creates us for a loving relationship with Himself; we are welcomed into the inner love and life of the Trinity.

Maybe our reasons for having children aren't so different. After all we still bear His image…

Conclusion

Life is very hard, yet God is very gracious to us throughout the course of it. It is a silly mistake to compare existence with non-existence, but I still prefer existence; without it we couldn't even make a category mistake. God has provided us with much beauty and enjoyment whether we believe in Him or not. Even when we do suffer seemingly pointless evil, He has given us the promise of His heaven to chase away the shadows of our suffering. God will birth a whole new world out of the old one when He renews all of creation. He has given us His guarantee through the death and resurrection of Jesus Christ and the deposit of His Holy Spirit in our hearts. What God did for Jesus on Easter Sunday, God will do for all of creation and for all those who repent and believe. According to scripture, our future state is not disembodied bliss. God will recreate our physical world and give us incorruptible resurrection bodies, and we will rule and reign with Him. Suffering, sorrow, sin, and the countless tears that result will be brushed away like a bad dream. We will awake at last to the beautiful reality that we've always longed for but have never had the words to describe. An unattainable ecstasy that has hovered enticingly over our entire existence will be ours at last.[28]

In the present perhaps we can't explain the existence of evil. It's possible that evil by its very nature does not make sense.[29] After all, sense is a part of our reason; our reason is a part of the image of God; and the image of God is a good thing. Evil is a corruption and soiling of the good, therefore, is evil perhaps irrational and beyond sense by definition? Regardless of how we answer that question the Bible[30] seems less concerned with why evil exists, or explaining its origin, than what God has done to address and deal with the problem. In the words of N.T. Wright:

> We are not told - or not in any way that satisfies our puzzled questioning - how and why there is radical evil within God's wonderful, beautiful and essentially good creation. One day I think we shall find out, but I believe we are incapable of understanding it at the moment, in the same way that a baby in the womb would lack the categories to think about the outside world. What we are promised, however, is that God will make a world in which all shall be well, and all manner of things shall be well, a world in which forgiveness is one of the foundation stones and reconciliation is the cement which holds everything together. And we are given this promise not as a matter of whistling in the dark, not as something to believe even though there is no evidence, but in and through Jesus Christ and His death and resurrection, and in and through the Spirit through whom the achievement of Jesus becomes a reality in our world and in our lives.[31]

This is the end of God's story and it is a happy one. The clouds of sin and sorrow that have gathered thickly and clung tenaciously to the soul of humanity will lift fully and finally; the light of God's Son will dispel the oppressive darkness. And all shall be well and all manner of things shall be well.

Quotes For Reflection

"Is everything sad going to come untrue? What's happened to the world?" (asked Sam). "A great shadow has departed," said Gandalf, and then he laughed, and the sound was like music, or like water in a parched land; and as he listened the thought came to him that he had not heard laughter, the pure sound of merriment, for days upon days without count. It fell upon his ears like the echo of all the joys he had ever known. But he himself burst into tears. Then, as sweet rain will pass down a wind of spring and the sun will shine out all the clearer, his tears ceased, and his laughter welled up, and laughing he sprang from his bed. "How do I feel?" he cried. "Well, I don't know how to say it. I feel, I feel" – he waved his arms in the air- "I feel like spring after winter, and sun on the leaves; and like trumpets and harps and all the songs I have ever heard!"[32]

What do you say to someone who is suffering? Some people are gifted with words of wisdom. For such, one is profoundly grateful. There were many such for us. But not all are gifted in that way. Some blurted out strange, inept things. That's OK too.

Your words don't have to be wise. The heart that speaks is heard more than the words spoken. And if you can't think of anything to say, just say, "I can't think of any-

thing to say. But I want you to know that we are with you in your grief." Or even, just embrace. Not even the best of words can take away the pain. What words can do is testify that there is more than pain in our journey on earth to a new day. Of those things that are more, the greatest is love. Express your love.[33]

THE BOOK OF JOB

A BRIEF REFLECTION

I received the call at 7:30 pm on a Friday night. Our small group had arrived at our home and we were settling comfortably into the evening's proceedings when the telephone rang. On the other end of the line was a police officer requesting my presence at the home of a family I know. Their brilliant, beautiful, talented 14-year-old son had taken his life after breaking up with his girl friend.

I still don't understand why he made that choice.

Why is it so difficult for young people to realize their current life doesn't have to be their forever life? A dark today doesn't have to cast a shadow on all of your tomorrows. A bad day never guarantees a horrible week, a horrible week doesn't necessitate a terrible month, a terrible month doesn't demand a traumatic year, and a traumatic year doesn't imply a brutal high school career. There are new beginnings in Jesus. Today is never forever.

That night, I walked into the house and sat with the family. I was present when they broke the news to an aunt and a grandmother. I watched those family members begin to process the tragedy. My heart hurt.

C.S. Lewis once wrote this about pain:

> "When I think of pain – of anxiety that gnaws like fire and loneliness that spreads out like a desert, and the heartbreaking routine of monotonous misery, or again

*of dull aches that blacken our whole landscape or sud-
den nauseating pains that knock a man's heart out at
one blow...it quite (overwhelms) my spirit."[1]*

The sudden, nauseating pains that knock a person's heart out
with one blow are not always physical. The tragic loss of a loved
one can steal our breath away, strike us in the stomach, flatten
our faith, beat down our buoyancy, and mire us in misery that
seems as unrelenting and inevitable as the endless march of time.

In that moment, my spirit felt overwhelmed. I will never forget
the cries of the 8-year-old sister, "I wish this was all just a dream,
I wish I could wake up, I wish that my brother was still here."
She choked out these words through sobs as her daddy lovingly
stroked her hair and whispered to her "I know honey, I know,
everything is going to be all right."

As a pastor certain moments get seared into your soul; this was
one of those moments. Several days later, at the celebration of
life, I read eulogies on behalf of the father and mother. I finished
reading the father's remembrance through tears, partly because I
have a little boy of my own.

What do you say in moments like these?

Many have fallen prey to the misguided 'mercy' of miserable
comforters. The sage who penned the Biblical book of Proverbs
was surely correct when he wrote, "The tongue of the wise brings
healing. The tongue of the fool brings harm." (Proverbs 12:18)

How do we comfort those who are afflicted? How do we avoid
trite answers and tired clichés? How do we 'testify' that there is
more than pain in our journey on earth to a new day?

Good questions.

We can learn much about how not to comfort those who are suffering by investigating the poor example of Job's friends.

The 'Comfort' Of Friends

Job, in the Biblical book named after him, experiences devastating hardship. His wealth is wiped out, his children are causalities of a 'freak' storm, his health deteriorates at an alarming rate, and his wife advises him to 'curse God and die'. Not great advice. Job has three friends who hear of his hardship and travel to comfort him.

> When Job's three friends, Eliphaz the Temanite, Bildad the Shuhite and Zophar the Naamathite, heard about all the troubles that had come upon him, they set out from their homes and met together by agreement to go and sympathize with him and comfort him. When they saw him from a distance, they could hardly recognize him; they began to weep aloud, and they tore their robes and sprinkled dust on their heads. They sat on the ground with him for seven days and seven nights. No one said a word to him, because they saw how great his suffering was. (Job 2:11-14)

There is much to be admired in Job's friends at this point in the narrative. This is certainly the case when contrasted with Job's family. At the end of the saga, when Job's fortunes are returned, we read, "After Job had prayed for his friends, the Lord restored his fortunes and gave him twice as much as he had before. All his brothers and sisters and everyone who had known him before came and ate with him in his house. They comforted and consoled him over all the trouble the Lord had brought on him, and each one gave him a piece of silver and a gold ring." (Job 42: 10,11) The reader is left wondering, where were these family members and friends earlier in the story, in the midst of the heart-ache and misery?

In our day we often hear sentiments like, 'true friends rush through the front door while the rest of the world frantically searches for the nearest exit.' Job's companions were available when his world went sideways; not to speak but simply to sit, to bear witness to his grief and share in it with him. This is a beautiful portrait of the ministry of presence, where we offer another person the gift of our time and nearness; expressing our love by sharing in the person's grief.

God is able to use us mightily in these moments of presence. Our time could be their tourniquet; our words, God's wisdom; our love, their lifeline; and our presence, God's smiling providence. And even if this is not the case, love compels us to be present.

Job's Friends Speak

Job's friends begin by sitting next to Job for seven days and nights. Unfortunately, this is not where they end. Job offers an agonizing lament in chapter 3 that begins, "May the day of my birth perish," (Job 3:3) and ends, "I have no peace, no quietness, I have no rest, but only turmoil." (Job3:26). Eliphaz the Temanite, Bildad the Shuhite and Zophar the Naamathite respond with a series of theological treatises on the nature of God and sin, and the manner in which our Creator runs the world. Here is a brief window into the 'comfort' offered by Job's advisors:

Job's sin is to blame for his suffering. (Job 4:7)

Suffering comes to the corrupt. (Job 5:3-5)

His problems are compounded by obstinacy. (Job 8:6)

His children sinned, that is why they died. (Job 8:4)

God will restore if you shape up. (Job 33:36)

Shocking! Appalling! These are reckless words that pierce like a sword; what presumption, what arrogance, what blind brutality is on display in the musings of these supposed friends.

Where did Job's comforters go wrong?

The Faults of Job's Friends

Job's friends tried to project their meaning, propped up by a skewed theological framework, onto Job's suffering. Their careless approach ignores the oft-repeated advice of modern day counselors that meaning shouldn't be imposed from without; to truly stick like stucco in the soul of the person, meaning must be created within the sufferer in their prolonged interaction with God and His word. Meaning in suffering is, I believe, an act of grace imparted by the Holy Spirit when the sufferer turns to God in desperation, and clings to God in the midst of desolation.

Not only do Eliphaz, Bildad, and Zophar impose their meaning on Job's suffering, it turns out to be the wrong meaning.

Job's friends offer the simple answer in response to Job's suffering, rooted in retribution theology: suffering is the result of sin. You are suffering, therefore, you are secretly sinning. Case closed. A logically valid argument, the conclusion flows necessarily and inescapably from the premises. Precise and to the point, yet emotionally devastating for, surely, if all specific suffering is the result of spectacular sin, the sufferer should be rebuked not comforted.

Job's friends had a distorted view of God's character and God's Word that erroneously connected all suffering with punishment for human transgression. Within scripture sin can and does lead to suffering, like smoking can and does lead to cancer, but not all who get cancer smoke and not all who suffer do so as a result of specific sin in their lives. We see that clearly by the end of the story of Job when God is angry with Job's companions for not speaking what is right (Job 42:7).

This simple truth gives room for a complex reality and helps us avoid simple-minded solutions or devastating inferences like those drawn by Job's friends, where the sufferer is rebuked instead of comforted.

All sin leads to some sort of suffering but not all suffering is the result of specific sin.

Simple answers, like those offered by Job's friends, often arise from insecure, fearful hearts that are uncomfortable with mystery. As Biblical scholar, Daniel Harrington writes, "The advice given by his friends seems superficial and proceeds from their own fear of suffering: "You see my calamity, and are afraid. (6:24)"[2] After all, if Job is righteous and he is still suffering that means that they may suffer even if they are righteous. They have no protection. One wonders if Job's friends desperately wanted their advice to be true; they hoped all suffering is connected to sin because avoiding sin would result in escaping suffering. In reality this is not the case. The causes of suffering are many and varied, and some of them are mysterious and known only to God and, potentially, Satan.

Suffering can be a harsh schoolmaster with more than one lesson to teach us throughout the course of our lives. For example, suffering can teach us that we are not in control; we are not the captains of our fate. I am not the sovereign 'I' to which the world must bow, to which the stars must align, and to which the morning sun must pay homage. Suffering robs us of all our delusions of grandeur and impresses on us the frailness of life; it can wean our hearts off the transitory nature of the world and push them towards finding rest in the secure, unchanging, eternal love of God.

Job's friends, however, are false prophets of reductionism. In their minds at least, the only lesson suffering has to teach is one of repentance. God's pedagogy involves pain, and suffering informs us that we have sinned. Learn the lesson by repenting and God's strict schoolmaster will go on vacation and you may once again enjoy your holiday of holiness and blessing. The book of Job rips a hole in the fabric of their theological framework because life with God is not that facile and straightforward; there are ambiguities, mysteries, and unwelcome uncertainties that grownups in the faith are forced to make peace with or, at the very least, declare an uneasy truce towards.

There is, after all no promise in scripture that we won't suffer evil that we don't understand and that we never saw coming; or sorrow that seemingly overwhelms our spirit and sucks dry our spiritual resources, leaving us gasping for air in a world that has plunged us under-water while simultaneously cutting off God's oxygen supply to our soul.

What the Scriptures do promise is that God will not allow us to undergo anything we can't handle with His help, that one day He will wipe away all tears, and that He will be forever with us and for us in the midst of whatever comes our way, good or bad. We are struck forcefully by this enduring truth at the end of Job's story.

Suffering Can Distort Reality

God is questioned incessantly throughout the course of Job's trials. With the arrival of chapter 38 it is God's turn to cross-examine Job. God thunders from the storm, "Will the one who contends with the Almighty correct Him? Let him who accuses God answer Him!"[3] Now, it is clear that suffering often warps and distorts our view of reality. Throughout the narrative, Job undertakes the role of the judge and God is on the docket. God is the one pummeled with questions. God is the one from whom Job demands an accounting for His running of the world.

God, however, reasserts the true nature of reality at the end of the book; God is the true judge and Job is on the docket. To quote Dr. Harrington again, "Whereas Job wants to make himself the center of the universe, God is offering Job a survey of how the cosmos looks from God's perspective."[4] When confronted with God's line of questioning in chapters 38 to 40 Job realizes that he can barely grasp how God runs the physical world, so who does he think he is in questioning God about His governing of the moral universe? Job's realization of this sobering fact is captured in these words:

> Then Job replied to the Lord: "I know you can do all things; no purpose can be thwarted. You asked, 'Who is this that obscures my plans without knowledge?' Surely I spoke of things I did not understand, things too wonderful for me to know."[5]

Many readers of Job react negatively to God's speeches at the end of the book, labeling them poetic and beautiful, but ultimately resulting in an unpersuasive non-answer. God appears as an insecure bully, beating Job into submission with an overwhelming display of His power and sovereignty. The above caricature is understandable, but it can also be argued in a reasonable fashion that God's response to Job reveals to us precisely what we need to know about evil and suffering. Here are a few noteworthy examples:

1. God's answer affirms that suffering and evil is often mysterious to us. We won't always understand why it occurs, or for what purpose God allows it. We will simply have to trust Him in the midst of it. This is true to our experience and, again, prevents us from drawing tenuous inferences from a person's difficulty or hardship to their personal transgressions, hidden or otherwise. In addition, this much-needed dose of humility prevents us from providing pat answers or textbook solutions, and drawing devastatingly direct lines of causation from a person's suffering to a person's sin. Embracing an element of mystery allows us to play the role of the pastor rather than the role of the prophet; comforting rather than confronting. We can come alongside and bring encouragement to those who endure unremitting evils, rather than criticism.

2. Evil is not out of God's control. This is crucial for us to understand. God is sovereign over evil. Evil cannot and does not thwart God's purposes. When addressing the problem of evil many writers attempt to affirm the reality of evil and God's goodness while denying His power and sovereignty. Job acknowledges God's sovereignty and the reality of evil but questions His goodness and justice. God responds by casting

strong doubts on Jobs' ability to make those types of moral pronouncements. Most striking, however, is the fact that Job begins and ends with a robust, overwhelming affirmation of God's sovereignty that extends to evil. All evil comes through God's hands, not through direct causation, but through secondary causes that He ultimately controls without, in some mysterious way, compromising His goodness and purity. We see that undeniably in the beginning of Job's story. This is hard to accept at first for sensitive souls, but it is Biblical and ultimately helpful. After all, to deny God's sovereignty over evil may get Him off the hook for suffering, but it inadvertently puts us on the hook of suffering. If God is not powerful enough to stop evil, He is not capable enough to overcome evil. What is meant to provide help by easing the intellectual pressure created by believing in God's goodness, power and evil simultaneously, ends up creating an existential crisis: God is as helpless as us in the face of evil. The end result is, I can't blame this God but I also can't bother this God for any meaningful outcome to sin, sorrow and suffering.

3. To state it simply, God is present with us. God is not unaware or unconcerned about our suffering. We will explore the relevancy of this stunning truth below.

God's Presence in Job

Theologian Douglas Hall once wrote,

> *Of answers to the 'problem of suffering' there is in fact no lack! Only, all of them flounder on the rocks of reality, at the cry of one starving or derelict child. The only satisfying answer is the answer given to Job – the answer that is no answer but is the presence of an Answerer.*[6]

God showed up at the end of Job's suffering, not with answers but with more questions. Yet, the presence of God was enough for Job. As author Philip Yancey writes,

> *The book of Job affirms that God is not deaf to our cries and is in control of this world no matter how it appears. God did not answer all of Job's questions, but God's very presence causes his doubts to melt away. Job learned that God cared about him intimately, and that God rules the world. That seemed enough.*[7]

Will it be enough for us? Job discovered that God cared about him, despite his disastrous circumstances. Where do we turn to have that same lesson carved deeply into the pliable tablet of our hearts? Throughout the pages of this book it has been suggested repeatedly that we must, sooner rather than later, arrive at the feet of the Savior. We should follow the Biblical trail from Job to Jesus, from a frightening storm to a forgotten stable, from a cyclone to a cruel cross.

In Job, God appears in a storm. In Jesus, God arrives in a stable.

In an act of breathtaking humility, God descended from a throne to a trough. Then, forsaken and rejected on a cross, God took upon Himself in Jesus the evils of our world and the just judgment our sins deserved.

This historical happening is captured beautifully in the Narnia book, *The Magician's Nephew*, where the Lion, Aslan, sings the pure, undefiled world of Narnia into existence only to have it, shortly thereafter, spoiled and sullied by unwelcome evil. Aslan, who is in the minds of many people a representation of Christ, responds to this tragic incursion of iniquity by gravely stating a profound promise:

> *"You see, friends," he said, "that before the new, clean world I gave you is seven hours old, a force of evil has already entered it; waked and brought hither by this son of Adam...But do not be cast down," said Aslan... "Evil will come of that evil, but... I will see to it that the worst falls upon myself."[8]*

In our world, as in the Narnia stories, the worst evil our world could offer, God allowed to fall upon Himself. For one brief moment on the cross Jesus, as our sin bearer, became God's enemy so that for the breadth of eternity we may be God's forgiven friends.

In giving His Son for us, God the Father gave His very heart to be trampled on by the careless soles and calloused souls of men.

This God knows what it is to lose His Son to the undeserved violence and evil of people. This God buried a Son if only to raise Him and, as a result, we can bury sons and daughters in hope that He will raise them to eternal life as well.

We can trust this suffering God in our own difficulty and loss. His tears can be our tourniquet, His suffering our salvation, His anguished cries our revelation of a God who is not aloof, or far off. This is a God who is with us in the blackest pit of unremitting sorrow and through the sharpest sting of nettling pain. In spite of the blasphemy and darkness of our hearts, Jesus is still our light; a beacon of God's love guiding us home to His heart even in the blackest night.

No Answers

On that difficult Friday evening, mourning together the tragic loss of a son who was beautiful and talented and intelligent, I had no words. I had no clever lines, no prophetic powers, and no wise insights to share. I read scripture, I prayed, I shared in the grief of the family. And when I read the eulogy I cried.

But I never had an answer.

Can we be placated without possessing all the answers in the face of horrific evil and suffering? Job was in the end. And, like Job, we may never have the answers to all our questions but we can know the Answerer. We may fail to fully understand why our lives run aground, spin off the tracks, capsize in the raging sea, or sputter into conflicting bundles of absurdity.

And often it can be this apparent lack of comprehension that creates a barrier of distrust between our heart and God's. Jesus alone is the bridge across that barrier. Because of Him we never have to make a choice between specific answers from God, or sustaining intimacy with God. Jesus is the ultimate answer from God who makes possible intimacy with God.

In the midst of suffering, the only tears that can ultimately provide comfort and shore up floundering faith, are tears on the 'face' of God. The other 'gods' have dry eyes, but every reader of the gospels has, at some point, stumbled across the wet cheeks apparent on Jesus' visage and had their soul leap to attention in salutation of a small but significant scripture, 'Jesus wept.' In the face of Jesus we glimpse the character of God, and there we find traces of His tender tears shed over a broken world. Wipe this God away from the horizon of our lives and we lose the healing balm of His tears and keep the biting bitterness of our own.

In the end, there is no solution to evil other than God's solution; no answer but His answer, and His Answerer is Jesus. Jesus brings the God we encounter in Job into sharper focus, and Jesus is the only God who would not only deserve worship in a world such as ours, but receive love and adoration as well, because in Jesus alone we find the God who is truly with us through the tempests of life.

So to end this journey where we began it; this book was never intended to heal; this book was written to reveal the God, who, in His perfect time, will do the healing.

His name is Jesus and He is still with you.

"I ended my first book with the words no answer. I know now, Lord, why you utter no answer. You are yourself the answer. Before your face questions die away. What other answer would suffice?"

– C.S. Lewis, *Till We Have Faces*

APPENDIX 1

A FEW WORDS ON NATURAL EVILS

Much of what I wrote in the later chapters of this book is directly applicable to sustaining faith in the face of horrific natural disasters. It is, however, worthwhile to venture a brief word about how Christians respond to natural evil through the free will defense or some type of soul-making theodicy.

Here are a few possible options:

Firstly, the existence of some natural evil is compatible with this world as a soul-making enterprise instituted by a God who desires to produce character, virtue and various other good (such as responsibility for one another) in His creatures.[1]

In order for the great good of soul-making to be obtained, freedom would be required, but God would also have to create a physical environment with certain law-like regularities within which moral agents (such as ourselves) could meaningfully interact.[2] This, of course, could explain some natural evil as the unfortunate bi-product of necessary natural processes (i.e. the same water that keeps us alive can drown us. The same nerve endings that allow us to experience pleasure also make intense pain possible etc).

Secondly, God may be confronted with various 'design constraints' that we are not altogether aware of that limit what He can accomplish given His other overriding purposes. Let me give you an example of what this could look like: At the core of our planet is molten iron, churning and bubbling, and it is this molten core that is responsible for continental drift and the earth-quakes that result when a drifting continent snags on another landmass; pressure builds up until the earthquake finally jolts it free and the plate continues it's slow, slow journey. As a result of the molten core we have earthquakes that cause incredible damage; we saw that in Haiti. So why didn't God create this planet without a molten core?

This molten iron core at the center of our planet also produces and sustains a magnetic field. The force of that field deflects much of the cosmic radiation coming from our sun, protecting our earth from lethal doses of these harmful rays. No molten core, no destructive earthquakes and some would live who have died. No molten core, no magnetic field and none of us would have ever lived.

Curious isn't it? No free will, no evil and no love. No nerve endings, no ability to feel physical pain and no ability to experience physical pleasure. No molten iron core, no earthquakes and no continents or life as we know it. Could God have done it differently? Perhaps, but in that alternate scenario we wouldn't be carbon-based creatures, or in other words, human beings.

Thirdly, if this world is a training ground for virtue, these natural evils, including diseases, can promote many opportunities to exercise compassion, sacrifice, ingenuity, bravery and responsibility for one another. Philosopher John Hick writes:

> *In a world devoid both of dangers to be avoided and rewards to be won, we may assume that virtually no development of the human intellect and imagination would have taken place, and hence no development of the sciences, the arts, human civilization, or culture.*[3]

As devastating as natural evils can be, they also provide a context for the greater good of social, technological and moral development to occur, evolve and progress.

Fourthly, many natural evils can be attributed to free will. Human choice is sometimes directly related to the disastrous effect of natural evils such as: disease caused by poor dietary habits or smoking; landslides resulting from the raping of the natural environment and irresponsible clear cutting; choosing to live near or on fault lines; building cities below water level, with insufficient protection and the knowledge that hurricanes often occur in the area; devastating famines when there is more than enough food; and unjust governments and poor building codes - all of which can cause disasters, or make them far more devastating than they need to be.

Think back to the Steve Jobs story and the starving children mentioned in the introduction of this book. The problem wasn't the lack of resources. God has created more than enough food to go around. The problem lies with human selfishness and greed. Sooner or the later the question for Jobs should have transitioned from, does God know about people starving, to, do we who have more than enough know about it and, if so, what are we doing to stop it?

Much more needs to be said here because the Christian could also invoke the doctrine of the fall (the world in its present state is not the way God originally made it – sin has had a pervasive, corrupting influence on the natural world), God sending calamity as judgment for human sin, or the activity of demonic creatures, thereby further extending the free will defense to cover all natural evils. In fact, when discussing harmful genetic mutations and suffering in the animal kingdom I am inclined to attribute these blights in God's good creation to demonic tampering prior to the fall of man. Though this may be unconvincing to the nonbeliever when it is the Christian worldview that is being questioned we may legitimately answer with the resources that our overarching narrative provides, including belief in demonic spirits.

Whatever approach the Christian takes to natural evils it is clear that many are made far more devastating by an abuse of human free will, and the resources for addressing the issue are many and varied within the Christian tradition. Regardless of our response to natural evils, the argument of this book remains: God's good-ness and power is not tarnished by permitting the possibility of natural evil in our experience if removing that potentiality would also eradicate some other greater good from our world, such as free will and soul-making (the process of growing to be more like Christ).

Moreover, if due to our limited perspective we are unable to per-ceive a greater good in the midst of frightful natural disasters, God has still given us reason enough to trust Him in the person of His Son and the sustaining presence of His Holy Spirit in the life of the believer. Perhaps this is why a surprising survey done in 2005 by the Washington Post after Hurricane Katrina, found out that when survivors who ended up as refugees in Houston, were asked about their faith in God, " Remarkably, 81% said the ordeal had strengthened their belief, while only 4% said it weakened it."[4] It seems that people would rather have the God revealed in Jesus together with the problem of evil in all of its varieties rather than no God and the pernicious problem of evil.

APPENDIX 2

At different points throughout the course of this work I have not been shy about mentioning that atheism can provide no ultimate hope in the face of evil. Atheism removes God, keeps evil, and creates the problem of hopelessness (see the Bertrand Russell quote in chapter 4). This statement is surely correct, but it opens up the possibility of the friendly atheist responding: Yes, what you say is true, but at least we are courageous enough to face the facts, as unfriendly as those facts may be. Our existence may be absurd, but we have the fortitude to embrace that absurdity and live our lives with dignity. At least we can't be accused of wish-fulfillment like you Christians. Your belief in heaven and cosmic justice and redemption is solely the result of your wishes and longings projected onto an otherwise cold and uncaring cosmos.

In this short appendix let me suggest how the Christian should respond to this popular but unsuccessful criticism.

The wish fulfillment argument is fallacious for many different reasons. Firstly, this 'argument' doesn't prove that there is no God. Rather, its burden is simply to show the inner consistency of atheism. The argument doesn't prove atheism; it presupposes atheism and, given that faith position, seeks to explain why many fellow 'primates' still believe in God. I assume the reasoning goes like this: There is no God yet many people believe in God. Why do so many individuals believe in a God that doesn't exist? Perhaps, people decide to create a God who provides hope, meaning, comfort and life after death. 'God' is fashioned in the familiar shape of our wants and needs; the image of a dad we never had.' I assume this is how the logic flows but, again, this type of reasoning doesn't prove atheism; it assumes atheism and then tries to explain away belief in God.

Secondly, this argument is a double-edged sword that cuts both ways. In fact, the wish fulfillment hypothesis implies that all worldviews, or overarching cultural narratives, are birthed out of human desires (collective or individual) and that would include atheism.[1] While writing this appendix, one of my Facebook friend's status update read: Stephen Hawking says, "Religion is for those afraid of the dark," John Lennox says, "Atheism is a fairy tale for those afraid of the light." That is the point exactly; witness the double-edged sword in action. After all, how do you know a person's belief that God doesn't exist isn't fueled by their desire to be an autonomous individual, or to live their life free from the entanglements of a meddlesome deity that presumes to interfere with their sexual proclivities - a desire to sidestep the light? Many atheists don't want there to be a God. Does that psychological fact alone prove that God actually exists? Of course, not! In the same way, longing for God to exist, or for life after death, doesn't imply that God doesn't exist, as the wish fulfillment argument would seem to suggest.

In fact, in our experience the opposite is often true. C.S. Lewis wrote long ago:

> *Creatures are not born with desires unless satisfaction for those desires exist. A baby feels hunger: well, there is such a thing as food. A duckling wants to swim: well, there is such a thing as water. Men feel sexual desire: well, there is such a thing as sex. If I find in myself a*

desire which no experience in this world can satisfy, the most probable explanation is that I was made for another world.[2]

In our human existence our desires often correspond to real objects or experiences that satisfy those desires. For the Christian our longing for God or eternity makes perfect sense. We desire God because we were created to know and enjoy God forever.

Thirdly, there are many elements of orthodox Christianity that I wouldn't wish for. For example, I don't relish the thought of hell for enemies or friends. In addition, Jesus' ethics found in the Sermon on the Mount certainly make life a little more difficult; learning to 'love my enemies' is not on my 'bucket list'.[3] Moreover, I would change some of the Ten Commandments and do away with uncomfortable religious duties like fasting. In my mind, the only type of "Christian" that can legitimately be accused of wish fulfillment is of the liberal variety that tends to jettison anything in scripture that doesn't jive with their personal proclivities, or the cultural moment in which they theologize. This theological liberalism is nothing but an exegetical hall of mirrors where different versions of oneself appear wherever one looks. Or to quote one last time the words of C.S. Lewis:

This [theological liberalism], by the way, exposes the feebleness of all those watered down versions of Christianity which leave out all the darker elements and try to establish a religion of pure consolation. No real belief in the watered down versions can last. Bemused and besotted as we are, we still dimly know at heart that nothing which is at all times and in every way agreeable to us can have objective reality.... Dream furniture is the only kind on which you never stub your toes or bang your knees.[4]

Dream furniture has a startling resemblance to dream theology. To believe and receive the whole counsel of scripture is a splash of cold water to the face, waking us up from our attempts at fashioning a God in our own image and likeness.

Fourthly, it is worth pointing out that the Freudian[5] wish fulfillment argument commits the 'genetic fallacy', which seeks to disprove a belief by showing how it originated. Even if belief in God fulfills human desires and needs, it doesn't, necessarily, follow that God doesn't exist.

In addition, throughout the course of this book we've hinted at a few reasonable arguments for God's existence, like the moral argument which could be stated as follows: 1. If objective moral values exist, God exists. 2. Evil exists. 3. Therefore, objective moral values exist. 4. But that entails that God exists.[6] In addition, religious experience and the resurrection of Jesus provide compelling reasons to believe in the existence of God.

Moreover, there is the Cosmological argument based on the beginning of the universe, which could be stated in a manner that explores the various explanatory options available for the existence of our universe and concludes that theism is the most reasonable. For example:

1. The universe was created by nothing from nothing.

2. The universe has always existed.

3. There are an infinite number of universes. As part of a larger world ensemble our universe may have come into existence, but the Multiverse, for all we know, is eternal.

4. God, or the 'gods' created the universe.

Responses:

1. Nothing when properly defined as non-being can't create something; that is a logical impossibility. Statement 1, therefore, is absurd.

2. Big Bang Cosmology has shown convincingly that the universe is not eternal. Rather, it came into existence at a certain point in the distant past. Statement 2, therefore, is unscientific, or at the very least embraces a position that doesn't represent the consensus of modern day cosmologists.

3. There is no empirical evidence for a Multiverse. The Multiverse is a bold metaphysical hunch that involves casting, without warrant, some of the traditional attributes and roles assigned to a supreme deity (eternal, powerful, creator) onto an unobservable physical reality. It is both a faith position and an egregious violation of Occam's Razor (i.e. the scientific principle that basically states, don't unnecessarily multiply explanatory entities. In other words, all things being equal, favour the simpler more elegant hypothesis for the observed phenomenon). Lastly, one could point out that it is easily within God's power to create an enormous number of universes.

CONCLUSION

As a result, when atheists are confronted with the question of why does something exist rather than nothing, the atheist is forced into a position that is either irrational, unscientific, or completely faith based.

Because we have other independent reasons to believe in God, the most reasonable conclusion is that God created the universe. The well-established scientific principle of Occam's Razor will dispose of any superfluous deities suggested by the skeptic, leaving us with one Supreme Being that must be spiritual, eternal, powerful and personal to have the will to create.

In addition, coinciding with the Cosmological argument is the Design argument resulting from the fine-tuning of the universe, which also provides a compelling reason to believe in a Creator.

Lastly, it is worth pointing out that theism appears to have greater success at accounting for significant facts of our existence including: objective morality, why something exists rather than nothing, religious experience in general, the reliability of our reason, the applicability of mathematics, our intuitive sense of free will, the fine-tuning of the universe, love, beauty, meaning, and truth.

But, alas, this is not a book on proofs for the existence of God. All I've given you are brief sketches of possible arguments for God's existence. If the reader is interested I would point them towards *Reasonable Faith* or *On Guard* by William Lane Craig, *I Don't Have Enough Faith to be an Atheist* by Frank Turek and Norman Geisler, or for the more advanced, *New Proofs for the Existence*

Chris Price

of God by Robert J. Spitzer, or *God and Other Minds* by Alvin Plantinga (See also Plantinga's lecture on *Two Dozen or so Good Arguments for the Existence of God*).

Regardless of the reader's interest in the above books, I believe the argument of this book has already succeeded in responding to the only compelling reason to deny God's existence: evil in our world.

The endnotes are important and informative. Give them a look.

Continue the conversation at *sufferingwithgod.com.*

E N D N O T E S

I N T R O D U C T I O N

1. Jeremiah 12:1

2. Sheldon Vanauken, A Severe Mercy, p. 192

3. Chapter 'Childhood', p. 24

4. It should also be noted that throughout this book I will employ a wide variety of words synonymous with evil, but, whether it be depravity, wickedness, sin, malfeasance or unrighteousness, I am still referring to evil as defined above in all of its ugly variety.

5. There are actually different versions of the logical argument. There is what I will refer to as the strict logical argument where the theist seeks to avoid the charge of an internal contradiction at the center of theism. In this approach the skeptic is trying to produce a contradiction between the following four propositions: A God exists who is 1. omnipotent 2. omniscient 3. benevolent and 4. evil exists. The skeptic then tries to prove that the believer can't hold to all of these beliefs in a consistent manner by bringing out other implicit premises in an attempt to prove an explicit contradiction at the center of the believer's position. If the skeptic can prove this argument they have dealt a death blow to the rationality of theism. This attempt, most impressively tried by the late J.L. Mackie, is almost universally recognized as a failed project. This is due, primarily, to the writings of the Christian philosopher Alvin Plantinga. Then there is the Evidentialist, or Probablistic version of the problem, where the skeptic concedes that evil and God's existence are logically possible, but the amount and gratuitous nature of evil makes the existence of God highly improbable. The most well-known proponent of this view would be the able atheist William Rowe. The above logical problems that evil creates for theism will be addressed either directly or indirectly, in the course of this book, but I don't wish to burden the reader with the numerous distinctions made throughout the philosophical literature.

6. Psalm 27:13

7. Daniel Howard-Synder, Reason for the Hope Within, p. 80

8. Millard J. Erickson, Christian Theology, pp. 599-617.

9. Many wonder if this rebellion occurred at the end of a long evolutionary process

after God breathed a spiritual awareness into the first Hominids. Some would contend that a historic fall from an original state of righteousness is incompatible with the theory of evolution. Yet, even if we grant the legitimacy of the evolutionary schema, it still seems possible to conceive of God breathing a spiritual awareness into the first Hominids at a certain point in their evolutionary development. Once our ancestors found themselves conscious of their Creator the choice of obedience or disobedience may have rushed forcefully to the front of their mind. Then the misuse of their will in disobeying God led to spiritual death because it cut them off from the source of all life – God Himself. Through Adam, therefore, all sin and all die. All inherit this sin nature because we can only reproduce what we are and our first parents were sinners alienated from their Creator. Though I don't grant the legitimacy of the entire evolutionary story, whatever the reader chooses to believe about the neo-Darwinian synthesis, or the historicity of Genesis one to three, one thing is apparent; the consequences of sin are still with us today. See God and Evolution edited by Jay Richards; Michael Behe, The Edge of Evolution, or Darwin's Black Box; Stephen Meyer, Signature in the Cell & Darwin's Doubt. For Christians supporting evolution see Dennis Alexander's Creation or Evolution: Do we have to Choose?; Francis Collins, The Language of God; or Darrel Falk, Coming to Peace with Science. It is, however, worth noting that embracing the entire theory of evolution, guided and intended by God, doesn't exacerbate the problem of evil as often suggested. Alvin Plantinga in his debate with Daniel Dennet makes several relevant comments on this issue. He writes,"Suppose we learn that our world, with all its problems, heartaches, and cruelty, will endure for millions of years before the advent of the new heaven and new earth; that wouldn't have much bearing, so one thinks, on the viability or satisfactoriness of this response to evil. (The new heaven and new earth, after all, will exist for a vastly longer period than our current sad and troubled old world.) But the same goes, I should think, for our learning that our world, with all it is heir to, has gone on much longer than originally thought. Current science shows that suffering, both human and animal, has gone on much longer than previously thought; but it doesn't thereby diminish the value of the Christian responses to the problem of evil and in this way doesn't exacerbate that problem much, if at all." Daniel C. Dennet & Alvin Plantinga. Science and Religion: Are they Compatible?

CHAPTER ONE

1. In the philosophical literature there is a common distinction made between a defense and a theodicy A defense seeks to avoid a contradiction between the propositions: A God exists who is omniscient, omnipotent and benevolent and evil exists by suggesting possible morally sufficient reasons that God may have for permitting evil. These suggested possibilities don't have to be true, believed personally by the defender, or even plausible, for the defender to diffuse the charge that there is an implicit contradiction that results from affirming all four of the above propositions. A theodicy, on the other hand, seeks to show the actual reason for God permitting the amount and atrocious nature of the many evils we encounter in our world. Throughout this chapter

we have sought to not burden the reader with this distinction, but for those interested we are developing a theodicy in this chapter that suggests that free will is one reason why God permits moral evil in His world. The reader may also wonder why I used the word 'defense' in the subheading if I am really suggesting a 'theodicy.' It is simply because the word 'defense' is more readily understood by the average reader than the word 'theodicy'. For those who know the difference I have included this generous footnote. You are welcome.

2. Throughout this chapter I am assuming libertarian free will, defined as the ability of human agents to act to the contrary in any given situation; it involves not just freedom to choose between our desires but freedom to form our desires. Our choices are, therefore, self-determined. This view of free will is accepted over and opposed to determinism, which contends that all actions are determined by heredity and environment; in this view we are simply dancing to our genes. Without an element of non-determinacy in human actions, the legitimacy of both moral praise-worthy deeds and morally reprehensible acts is destroyed. There is, of course, a third view adopted by some Calvinists and philosophers called compatibilism. D.A. Carson in his wonderful book, 'How Long O Lord?' explains compatibilism this way:

> God is absolutely sovereign, but his sovereignty never functions in such a way that human responsibility is curtailed, minimized, or mitigated.
>
> Human beings are morally responsible creatures – they significantly choose, rebel, obey, believe, defy, make decisions, and so forth, and they are rightly held accountable for such actions; but this characteristic never functions so as to make God absolutely contingent. See Genesis 50:19,20, Leviticus 20:7-8, 1st Kings 8:46, Isaiah 10:5, John 6:37-40 and Acts 4:23-32, 18:9-10 for apparent Biblical support.

If this is compatiblism than I have no qualms with it. However, often compatiblism is worked out (philosophically) in a way that ends up sharing many of the same problems that plague the determinist position; it certainly tends to exacerbate the problem of evil. Simply stated, compatibilism is the freedom to act on our strongest desire, or to say it another way, 'freedom is an un-coerced action'. As long as our action is un-coerced, it is free. This position, however, doesn't allow you to do anything other than what you did which seems to destroy moral accountability as well as not adequately describing our intuitive moral experience. The Calvinist would respond that compatibilism is the Biblical view. However, this remains a very controversial assertion. For example, "No temptation has overtaken you except what is common to mankind. And God is faithful; He will not let you be tempted beyond what you can bear. But when you are tempted He will also provide a way out so that you can endure." (1st Corinthians 10:13) If this scripture (and many others like it) have any coherent meaning they seem to provide the deathblow to both determinism and compatabilism (see Chosen but Free by Normal Geisler or Why I am not a Calvinist by Jerry Walls). I don't, of course, feel required by libertarian freewill to embrace Open Theism as a solution to the problem of evil as some have done (see Gregory Boyd Is God to Blame?). We ascribe to libertarian freedom because we believe the Bible assumes something akin to it and it appears necessary for morality to be a meaningful category in our human experience. We oppose open theism because the Bible clearly denies its central tenet (the future is unknowable even to God) while simultaneously affirming God's sovereignty over the future and evil. Any theodicy that resorts to open theism is, in the opinion of this author, sub-Biblical (at least on this point). See Richard Swinburne, The Providence of God and Evil: which is a great example of this type of failure.

3. C.S. Lewis makes this point in The Problem of Pain, p. 16

4. See Alister McGrath, God and Suffering, pp. 21-26 for a short but fascinating discussion of these matters.

5. See Alvin Plantinga, God and Other Minds, pp. 168-173

6. It is, of course, important to note that we aren't required to know all that is intrinsically possible for the free will defense to succeed. We simply need knowledge of what is intrinsically impossible like contradictions.

7. Norman Geisler, If God, Why Evil? p. 62

8. C.S. Lewis, Mere Christianity, p. 65

9. D.A. Carson, How Long O Lord?: Reflections on Suffering and Evil, p. 189

10. William Lane Craig & Walter Sinnot Armstrong, God ? A Debate Between a Christian and an Atheist, p. 116

11. A similar comment could be made regarding the punishment theodicy, the soul-making theodicy, or the natural law theodicy.

12. Michael Ruse, Can a Darwinian be a Christian? p. 170

13. "Darwinism by itself did not produce the Holocaust, but without Darwinism... neither Hitler nor his Nazi followers would have had the necessary scientific underpinnings to convince themselves and their collaborators that one of the world's greatest atrocities was really morally praiseworthy." - Richard Weikart, From Darwin to Hitler: Evolutionary Ethics, Eugenics, and Racism in Germany

14. "My firm conviction is that if wide-spread Eugenic reforms are not adopted during the next hundred years or so, our Western Civilization is inevitably destined to such a slow and gradual decay as that which has been experienced in the past by every great

ancient civilization. The size and the importance of the United States throws on you a special responsibility in your endeavours to safeguard the future of our race. Those who are attending your Congress will be aiding in this endeavour, and though you will gain no thanks from your own generation, posterity will, I believe, learn to realize the great debt it owes to all the workers in this field." - Leonard Darwin

15. David Hume (1739), A Treatise of Human Nature, p. 335. The problem involves trying to draw imperative conclusions from indicative premises (this is contested, of course, in the philosophical literature). Hume, however, thought this was impossible. John Lennox adds: "Furthermore, in claiming that there was no rational basis for ethics in nature, Hume pointed out that, in the first place, nature tended to give conflicting signals, and secondly, and more importantly, to attempt to deduce ethics from nature was to commit a category mistake: observations in nature are first-order activities, whereas value judgments are second-order; that is, they do not belong in the same category." John C. Lennox, Gunning for God: Why the New Atheists are Missing the Target.

16. Gregory Koukl & Beckwith J. Francis, Relativism: Feet Firmly Planted in Mid Air. Baker Books: Grand Rapid, Michigan, 1998, p. 63

17. C.S. Lewis, The Poison of Subjectivism: The Collected Works of C.S. Lewis, p. 226

18. C.S. Lewis Mere Christianity, p. 31

19. Cornelius G. Hunter, Darwin's God, p. 154

20. I am quoting myself here. I hope the reader can forgive my presumption.

CHAPTER TWO

1. As quoted in Philip Yancey, Disappointment with God, pp. 252, 253.

2. This, of course, opens the believer up to charges of wish fulfillment from the atheist. See Appendix 2 for my response.

3. I first heard a version of this parable in the television drama West Wing season number two.

4. C.S. Lewis, Mere Christianity p. 140

5. Blaise Pascal said something like this somewhere

6. John 1:1-18

7. This analogy was first suggested to me by a Timothy Keller talk he gave at Google

in New York. He, however, referenced Dorothy Day writing herself into one of her novels. This analogy is also employed to great effect by Sheldon Vanauken in A Severe Mercy, p. 133,134. I have, of course, tweaked it to suit my purposes, but it most nearly resembles Vanauken's use of it in A Severe Mercy.

8. See John 10:18

9. John 3:16

10. 1 John 4:9-10

11. Timothy Keller, The Reason for God, p. 31

12. John 15:13

13. Romans 5:8

14. Romans 8:37-39

15. I heard this line from Ravi Zacharias somewhere.

16. Editor Michael L. Peterson. Redemptive Suffering: A Christian Solution to the Problem of Evil by Marilyn M. Adams. The Problem of Evil: Selected Readings, p. 179

17. Ron Dunn, When Heaven is Silent, pp. 69-75

18. I once heard a speaker make this point but I have shortened what he said into one succinct sentence here.

19. Matthew 6:14-15

20. 1 Corinthians 13:13

21. Dorothy L. Sayers, "The Greatest Drama Ever Staged," in The Whimsical Christian, p. 12

22. God, of course, is morally perfect and there is no sin or evil that can be legitimately charged to Him. Therefore, God cannot be a meaningful object of our forgiveness. Why the above line then? Simply because there are many people who carry bitterness in their heart against God as a result of suffering and, before they can grow and heal, they will have to let that go in a manner that can 'feel' like forgiveness. But part of the person's letting go will involve repentance on their part for wrongly holding bitterness against God.

23. From a letter to written by C.S. Lewis to Miss Breckenridge, 19 April 1951

24. Richard Swinburne, Is there a God? Revised Edition, p. 111

25. C.S. Lewis, Prayer Letters to Malcolm, Letter 18

26. This first appeared on the blog groundedinthegospel.com. Since then I have made several modifications.

27. Steve Kroeker is lead Pastor at Tsawwassen Alliance. This blog was originally posted on groundedinthegospel.com.

CHAPTER THREE

1. In the Sherlock Holmes movie a miracle did not occur. Moreover, if Holmes and Watson had readily believed in a miracle and not investigated the issue more thoroughly the truth of the matter would not have surfaced. In this way, citing this movie could be counter productive for my purposes because the skeptic could use it against me as well. So let me be clear: I used the example of Holmes and Watson solely because they were at least open to a supernatural explanation and many today are not. They were open to following the evidence where it led. If God exists, miracles are possible. I think the evidence surrounding the resurrection of Jesus is best explained by a miracle. That is where the evidence leads – the only question is, are we open minded enough to follow it?

2. John Stott, The Cross of Christ, pp. 335, 336

3. N.T Wright, Surprised by Hope, p. 36. Wright also points out that resurrection in 1st century Judaism was not a euphemism for life after death. Rather, resurrection referred to life after life after death.

4. It is well known that the Sadducees did not, in fact, believe in the resurrection but the Pharisees certainly did.

5. For a fuller study on the resurrection of Jesus see: N.T. Wright, The Resurrection of the Son of God; Michael R. Licona, The Resurrection of Jesus: A New Historiographical Approach; Gary Habermas, The Risen Jesus & Future Hope. Jesus' Resurrection: Fact or Fiction. A Debate between William Lane Craig & Gerd Ludemann edited by Paul Copan. The Resurrection of Jesus: John Dominic Crossan and N.T Wright in Dialogue, edited by Robert B. Stewart.

6. To quote N.T. Wright: "It must be asserted most strongly that to discover a particular writer has a bias tells us nothing whatever about the value of the information he or she presents. It merely bids us be aware of the bias (and our own, for that matter), and to assess the material according to as many sources as we can." N.T. Wright, The New Testament People of God, p. 89

7. Scholar Craig Blomberg points this out in Real Answers: Jesus, the Search Continues (produced for Inspiration Network), Tape 1. A transcript of this video series is available at www.insp.com/jesus/transcipts.htm.

8. My editor astutely pointed out that members of the French underground during WW2 would lie to keep the truth from the Nazis, and die defending that lie in order to conceal the truth. This situation, however, is much different from the one faced by the first disciples of Jesus. What would the disciples have been concealing? That Christianity is a hoax? Why would they do that? That type of deception wouldn't help themselves or anyone else? No lives would be spared by that lie only wasted, spent frivolously propagating falsehoods until they were silenced by death. Not only that, theologically speaking, the disciples believed that liars can go to hell. So what would they gain through the deception? Sane people die for noble reasons like those members of the French Underground, but this is not similar to the disciples situation. Moreover, the above statement has to be taken in conjunction with all the other information we have about 1st century Judaism and the options it provided the first disciples with after Jesus was crucified (i.e. go home or find another messiah). There was no need to make up a new religion and then die for that lie.

9. William Lane Craig, The Son Rises, p. 24

10. Simon Greenleaf, The Testimony of the Evangelists: The Gospels Examined by the Rules of Evidence Administered in Courts of Justice, p. 32

11. Francis J. Beckwith, "History & Miracles", in Defense of Miracles, R. Douglas Gievett & Gary R. Habermas (Eds).

12. See N.T. Wright, The Resurrection of the Son of God: or William Lane Craig, The Son Rises.

13. Francis J. Beckwith, "History & Miracles", in Defense of Miracles, R. Douglas Gievett & Gary R. Habermas (Eds).

14. In addition, we cannot claim for ourselves any sort of safeguard against the miraculous based on an assumed uniformity of nature (or in other words, the weighty testimony of nature against miracles occurring), as the famous skeptic David Hume seems to have done in his centuries old argument against miracles. C.S. Lewis correctly pointed out contra Hume: "We know the experience against (miracles) to be uniform only if we know that all reports of them are false. And we can know all the reports to be false only if we know already that miracles have never occurred. In fact, we are arguing in circles." (C.S. Lewis, Miracles, p. 162.) You see, if there is a God this God could certainly act in history. To claim otherwise is to assume, without argument, the truth of atheism. And in the end, probability comes into play when assessing whether or not an alleged miracle took place in history but it is not the determining factor.

History, after all, is riddled with improbable, onetime events, and we don't determine truth by the odds but by the facts. Otherwise, we wouldn't be able to believe in the resurrection even if it did happen!

15. As J.P. Moreland writes, the "differences far outweigh the similarities. The mystery religions have a consort, a female deity who is central to the myth. They have no real resurrection, only a crude resuscitation. The mysteries have little or no moral context, fertility being what the mystery rites sought to induce. The mysteries are polytheistic, syncretistic legends unrelated to historical individuals…the majority of sources which contain parallels with Christianity are dated after the Christian faith was established. This fact, coupled with the fact that the mystery religions were syncretistic, shows that if any borrowing went on, the mysteries borrowed from Christianity and not vice versa." J.P. Moreland, Scaling the Secular City, p. 182.

16. This group of scholars was called the Religionsgeschichtliche schule, which flourished at the end of the nineteenth century and into the early twentieth century. By the mid-twentieth century, scrupulous scholars had convincingly shown that the sources employed by this school of thought were unsatisfactory and the parallels were overdrawn and largely superficial. Lee Strobel, The Case for the Real Jesus, p. 167

17. See Lee Strobel, The Case for the Real Jesus, pp. 157-187. In these pages Lee Strobel interviews noted expert in Mithraic studies, Edwin M. Yamauchi, who debunks these unsubstantiated comparisons between Christianity and the pagan mystery religions.

18. 1 Corinthians 15:3-8

19. Despite my quoting of the scripture above, nothing I write in this chapter assumes the divine inspiration of the scripture (though I believe in it). The case I'm building in this chapter is valid even if the New Testament Gospels should be riddled through with historical errors. So let's lay aside our adopted dogmas (secular or religious) and put on our detective hats to examine the eyewitness testimony and various strands of circumstantial evidence.

20. Norman Geisler & Ravi Zacharias Who Made God? p. 99

21. Atheist Richard Dawkins writes, "Usually when we hear a miracle story it's not from an eye-witness, but from somebody who heard about it from somebody else, who heard it from somebody else, who heard it from somebody else's wife's friend's cousin…and any story, passed on by enough people, gets garbled." Firstly, I have heard about miracles involving dramatic healings, directly from eyewitnesses. Secondly, Dawkins' comments are irrelevant when it comes to 1 Corinthians 15. See Richard Dawkins, The Magic of Reality, p. 239

22. N.T. Wright, The Resurrection of the Son of God

23. N.T. Wright, Surprised by Hope, p. 47

24. N.T. Wright, Surprised by Hope, p. 62; Gary Habermas & Michael Licona The Case for the Resurrection, p. 71

25. N.T. Wright, Surprised by Hope, p. 62

26. Josephus Jewish Antiquities 20:20

27. See Michael Licona, The Resurrection of Jesus, pp. 108-111

28. Michael Licona, The Resurrection of Jesus, p. 617. Licona interacts with Gerd Ludemann, Michael Goulder, John Dominic Crossan, Geza Vermes and Peter Crafferts throughout this work.

29. This explanation was put forward by Gerd Ludemann.

30. See Gary Habermas and Michael Licona, The Case for the Resurrection of Jesus.

31. Similar criticisms can be applied in a devastating manner to another popular option employed to explain the alleged resurrection appearances: the disciples had some type of rich spiritual experience, which they interpreted through Jewish modes of thought. This doesn't explain the empty tomb, why they used the terminology of resurrection when, within Judaism, there was other more appropriate language available and it doesn't explain the conversion of skeptics like Paul and James. All of these various explanations lack explanatory power and explanatory scope, as well as displaying a marked deficiency when it comes to illumination and plausibility.

32. Michael R. Licona, The Resurrection of Jesus, p. 619

33. 1 Corinthians 15

34. To some readers this might seem like a natural move for the first Christians to make as the Gospel message spread throughout the Greek world, especially after the Jewish Temple was destroyed by the Romans. But, again, the first Christians were Jewish, and many of them made this unprecedented break with Jewish tradition as soon as they clearly understood the implications of what Christ had accomplished on their behalf. This represents a seismic shift in religious understanding which, in their understanding, would have put at risk the damnation of their souls. They believed a new stage of redemptive history had been inaugurated through Jesus, the Gentiles were being welcomed into God's fold, the law had been fulfilled, the Spirit had been given; all this in light of a crucified Messiah. This is very hard to understand apart from the resurrection of Christ providing God's stamp of approval on the life, death and ministry of Jesus.

35. The 'new properties' referred to by N.T. Wright in this quote would likely include, the imperishable nature of Jesus' body (raised never to die again), and its uncanny ability to walk through walls.

36. Ibid, pg. 63, 64

37. C.S. Lewis makes this comment towards the end of his book Miracles.

38. Galatians 4:4, 5

39. Nicholas Wolterstorff, Lament for a Son, p. 92

40. Mark Buchanan, Things Unseen, pp. 231-236

41. This is Mark Buchanan's phrase.

42. In case the reader supposes that belief in the resurrection of Jesus is an absurd act of blind faith, let me point you to several books that contend for the historicity of Jesus' resurrection. See: William Lane Craig, The Son Rises; Gary Habermas and Michael Licona, The Case for the Resurrection of Jesus; N.T. Wright, The Resurrection of the Son of God; and Michael Licona, The Resurrection of Jesus.

43. Pastor David Smith of Crossway Church in Surrey. This blog was originally posted on the site groundedinthegospel.com.

44. It should be mentioned that when babies miscarry in the first trimester it is usually because something was wrong with the fetus. For example, there was no heart, the brain was not developing, or the little one wouldn't connect to the endometrium to be nourished etc. In this sense miscarriages can prevent a child from having a miserable existence or dying at birth, which would be much more traumatic for the parent. This thought should not be shared with someone who has miscarried and the integrity and helpfulness of David's story remains intact. We do, however, have to be careful about looking only at the negatives of miscarriage, especially when you lose a child in first term. This type of reasoning, however, cannot be used to support abortion. In a miscarriage God takes the child home to heaven. In abortion we play God. Again, if God doesn't take the child home we have no right to send the child to meet God by killing the fetus.

CHAPTER FOUR

1. Romans 8:18

2. Bertrand Russell, Mysticism and Logic, pp. 47-49

3. C.S. Lewis, The Problem of Pain, pp. 148, 149

4. 2nd Corinthians 2:5, 6

5. Genesis 1, 1st Corinthians 15 (whole chapter), Romans 8:19-24, Revelation 21:1-5

6. Darrell Johnson, Discipleship On The Edge.

7. Revelation 21:1-3

8. For more detailed research on the book of Revelation see: Darrell Johnson, Discipleship on the Edge; Robert W. Wall Revelation: New International Biblical Commentary; Paul Spilsbury, The Throne, The Lamb & The Dragon; Richard Bauckham, The Theology of the Book of Revelation; Leon Morris, Revelation: The Tyndale New Testament Commentaries; Eugene Peterson, Reversed Thunder: The Revelation of St. John & the Praying Imagination; George Eldon Ladd, A commentary on the Revelation of John; or Bruce Metzger, Breaking the Code.

9. See When the Kings come Marching by Richard J. Mouw, or Discipleship on the Edge by Darrell Johnson

10. I have heard several preachers say this. I wonder if Darrel Johnson was the first to make this point in this way.

11. See Marilyn McCord Adams, Horrendous Evils and the Goodness of God.

12. Romans 8:8

13. My friend Andy Steiger from Apologetics Canada likes to make this point.

14. C.S. Lewis, The Last Battle, p. 228

15. This represents an accurate summary of the dialogue between Jay and Manny, not a word for word transcription.

16. I adapted this analogy from a sermon given by Mark Driscoll on 1st John chapter 4. See, www.marshillchurch.com. I've changed it slightly and added more details.

17. Check out Jon at jonmorrison.ca

18 C.S. Lewis, The Problem of Pain, pp. 118,119

19. When it comes to this emotionally loaded topic I am mindful of the apostle Paul's warning in 2nd Timothy 4:3 where he writes, "For the time will come when people will not put up with sound doctrine. Instead, to suit their own desires, they will gather around them a great number of teachers to say what their itching ears want to hear." This is a dangerous tendency. We have an innate propensity to find compelling teachers who tell us what we want to hear. Our emotions can transform our exegesis into

eisegesis if we are not careful. Though it may not be my business, I wonder if this tendency is at work in the hearts of those who embrace this modified understanding of hell. But you can decide for yourself because I don't think we will settle the issue in this conversation.

20. Peter Kreeft & Ronald K. Tacelli, Handbook of Christian Apologetics, p. 300

21. Peter Kreeft & Ronald K. Tacelli, Handbook of Christian Apologetics, p. 300

22. This type of pastoral response to Brandon's question was suggested to me by Dr. Paul Chamberlain, who gave credit to Ravi Zacharias.

23. C.S. Lewis, The Problem of Pain, p. 116

24. C.S. Lewis, Mere Christianity, pp. 136, 137

25. This last image is borrowed from C.S. Lewis' essay Meditations in a Woodshed.

26. William Lane Craig, Hard Questions, Real Answers, p. 100.

27. This whole dialogue can also be seen as an exposition of this statement: "If I am glad on the whole about my own existence and that of persons close to me, then I cannot reproach God for the general character or the major events of the world's past history." (Michael L. Peterson, God and Evil: An Introduction to the Issues, p. 120) The above statement is, of course, the result of serious argumentation, but even without the argumentation the proposal has a prima facie plausibility to me. In addition, this dialogue has some relevance to the probabilistic version of the problem of evil because probability is always relative to total evidence, or background information. This dialogue brings into the conversation much of the background information that makes belief in God still plausible in light of the atrocious evils in our world.

28. For those who might say no future bliss, no redemptive act of God, can make up for temporal suffering we've endured, the words of C.S. Lewis are appropriate: "They say of some temporal suffering, 'No future bliss can make up for it,' not knowing that Heaven, once attained, will work backwards and turn even that agony into a glory."

29. This was pointed out to me by Christopher Wright in his book, The God I Don't Understand.

30. In Bart Erhman's book, God's Problem: How the Bible Fails to Answer Our Most Important Question – Why We Suffer, he does a fairly decent job of summarizing the various Biblical approaches to the issue of suffering. He also constantly hits his readers over the head with the many types of evils that are widespread on our planet. Once reading the end of the book, however, you realize the main reason why Erhman doesn't think the Bible answers the problem of evil and suffering is that he doesn't believe the

Bible. If he actually believed the Bible he would find more than enough intellectual and emotional resources to overcome the problem of evil. In the end the book would be more appropriately titled 'Bart Erhman's Problem'. God has addressed the issue in His Word.

31. N.T. Wright, Evil and the Justice of God, p. 164

32. J.R.R. Tolkien, "The Field of Cormallen," chapter in The Lord of the Rings: The Return of the King (various editions).

33. Nicholas Wolterstorff, Lament For A Son, p. 34

THE BOOK OF JOB

1. C.S. Lewis, The Problem of Pain, p. 105

2. Daniel Harrington, Why Do We Suffer? A Scriptural Approach to the Human Condition, p. 37

3. Job 40:2

4. Daniel Harrington, Why Do We Suffer? A Scriptural Approach to the Human Condition, p. 45

5. Job 42:2,3

6. Douglas John Hall God & Human Suffering: An Exercise in the Theology of the Cross, p. 118

7. Philip Yancey, The Bible Jesus Read, p. 68

8. C.S. Lewis, The Magician's Nephew , p. 80

APPENDIX 1

1. See John Hick, Evil and the Love of God. Hick argues powerfully for the 'soul making' theodicy while also employing some elements of the free will defense. He traces his theodicy back all the way to the early church father Irenaeus. The Biblical Christian, however, will likely not be pleased with his understanding of sin and the fall. Firstly, he denies the historic doctrine of the fall based on current evolutionary theory which seems to be an unwarranted dismissal. Secondly, he seems to insinuate that the fall was directly caused by God's primary agency for the purpose of redemption and soul making. In this theodicy, it seems like God is directly the cause of evil.

2. See C.S. Lewis, The Problem of Pain, pp. 21-23 for a powerful presentation of this idea.

3. John Hick, "An Irenaean Theodicy", in Encountering Evil, Stephen T. Davis (Ed.), p. 46

4. Randy Alcorn, If God is Good? p. 406

APPENDIX 2

1. Atheists will insist aggressively that atheism is not a worldview, or even a belief. I would simply respond, 'Yes it is,' and I would invite any one to read the writings of popular atheists. It won't take long to discover their shared assumptions that shape their view of reality rooted directly in their commitment to a godless universe and a false dichotomy between God and science and an out of date epistemology.

2. C.S. Lewis, Mere Christianity, pp. 137, 138.

3. A pop culture reference to a popular movie called The Bucket List. A bucket list is a list of experiences that you want to have before you 'kick the bucket', or die.

4. C.S. Lewis, Prayer Letters to Malcolm. Letter 14

5. See Future of an Illusion by Sigmund Freud.

6. Philosopher William Lane Craig often argues the Moral Argument in this manner.

BIBLIOGRAPHY

Adams McCord, Marilyn. *Horrendous Evils and the Goodness of God*. Cornell University Press: Ithaca, NY, 1999.

Adams McCord, Marilyn. *Christ and Horrors: The Coherence of Christology*. Cambridge University Press: England, 2006.

Alcorn, Randy. *If God is good?* Multnomah Books, Colorado Springs, Colorado, 2009.

Alcorn, Randy. *Heaven*. Tyndale House Publishers: Carol stream, Ill, 2004.

Alexander, Dennis. *Creation of Evolution: Do we have to choose?* Monarch Books: Grand Rapids, Michigan, 2008.

Ancient Christian Writers: *St. Augustine's. Faith, Hope and Charity*. Newman Press, New York

Ancient Christian Writers: St. Augustine. *Freedom of the Will*. Newman Press, New York.

Bagget, David & Walls L. Jerry. *Good God*. Oxford University Press: Oxford, England, 2011.

Baker, Don. *Pain's Hidden Purpose: Finding Perspective in the Midst of Suffering*. Multnomah Press: Portland, Oregon, 1984.

Behe, Michael. *Darwin's Black Box*. Free Press: New York, NY, 2006.

Boyd A, Gregory. *Is God to Blame?* Intervarsity Press: Downers Grove, Illinois, 2003.

Boethius. *The Consolations of Philosophy*. Penguin Books: New York, NY, first published 1969.

Blocher, Henri. *Evil and the Cross*. Kregel Publications: Grand Rapids MI, 1994.

Buchanan, Mark. *Things Unseen*. Multnomah Publishers: Sisters, Oregon, 2002.

Billheimer E. Paul. *Don't Waste your Sorrows: Finding God's Purpose in the Midst of Pain*. Bethany House Publsihers: Minneapolis, MN, 1977.

Carson, D.A. *How long O lord: Reflections on Suffering and Evil*. Baker Academic: Grand Rapids, Michigan, 2006.

Carson, D.A. *Divine Sovereignty & Human Responsibility: Biblical Perspectives in Tension*. Wipf and Stock Publishers: Eugene, Oregon, 1994.

Craig, L. William. *Hard Questions, Real Answers*. Crossway Books: Wheaton, Illinois, 2003.

Craig, L. William. *The Son Rises: The Historical Evidence for the Resurrection of Jesus*. Wipf and Stock Publishers: Eugene, Oregon, 1981.

Craig, L. William & Moreland, J.P. *Philosophical Foundations of a Christian Worldview*. InterVarsityPress: Downers Grove, Ill, 2003.

Copan, Paul. *Is God a Moral Monster?* Baker Books: Grand Rapids, Michigan, 2011.

Coyne A. Jerry. *Why Evolution is True*. Penguin Books: New York, NY, 2009.

Chan, Francis & Sprinkle, Preston. *Erasing Hell: What God said about eternity, and the things we've made up*. Published by David C. Cook: Colorado Springs: CO, 2011.

Chamberlain, Paul. *Can we be good without God?* Intervarsity Press, Downers Grove, Illinois, 1996.

Chesterton. G.K. *Orthodoxy*. Moody Publishers: Chicago, Illinois, 2009 Edition

Daniel C. Dennet & Alvin Plantinga. *Science and Religion: Are they Compatible?* Oxford University Press: New York, NY, 2011.

Dawkins, Richard. *The God Delusion.* Houghton Mifflin Company: New York, NY, 2006.

Dawkins, Richard. *The Blind Watchmaker.* Penguin Books: London, England, 1986.

Dawkins, Richard. *The Magic of Reality.* Free Press: New York, NY, 2011.

Dawkins, Richard. *The Devil's Chaplain.* Houghton Mifflin: Boston, Mass. 2003.

Dembski A. William. *The End of Christianity: Finding a Good God in an Evil World.* B & H Publishing Group: Nashville, Tennessee, 2009.

Epstein, M. Greg. *Good without God.* HarperCollins publisher: San Francisco, CA, 2009.

Edited by Jay Richards. *God and Evolution.* Discovery Institute Press: Seattle, WA, 2010.

Edited by Nevin c. Norman. *Should Christians Embrace Evolution?* InterVarsity Press: Nottingham, England, 2009.

Edited by Willem B. Drees. *Is Nature ever Evil?* Routledge Publisher: New York, NY, 2003.

Edited by Francis J. Beckwith, J.P Moreland, William Lane Craig. *To Everyone an Answer.* Intervarsity Press, Downers Grove, Illinois. 2004.

Edited by Geivett R. Douglas & Habermas R. Gary. *In Defense of Miracles: A Comprehensive Case for God's Action in History.* Intervarsity Press: Downers-Grove, Ill, 1997.

Edited by Meister, Chad & Dew K. James. *God and Evil: The Case for God in a World Filled with Pain.* IntervarsityPress: Downers Grove, Ill. 2013.

Edited by John W. Loftus. *The Christian Delusion: Why Faith Fails.* Prometheus Books: Amherst, NY, 2010

Edited by Daniel Howard Synder. *The Evidential Argument from Evil.* Indiana University Press: Bloomington, IN, 1996.

Edited by Michael J. Murray. *Reason for the Hope Within.* William B. Eerdman's Publishing Company: Grand Rapids, MI, 1999.

Editor Robert B. Stewart. *The Future of Atheism: Alister McGrath & Daniel Dennet in Dialogue.* Fortress Press: Minneapolis, 2008.

Edited by Marilyn McCord Adams & Robert Merrihew Adams. *The Problem of Evil.* Oxford University Press: Oxford, England, 1990.

Edited by John Piper & Justin Taylor. *Suffering and the Sovereignty of God.* Crossway Books: Wheaton, Ill, 2006.

Erhman, Bart. *God's Problem.* HarperCollins Publishing: New York, NY, 2008.

Feinberg S. John. *The Many Faces of Evil.* Crossway Books: Wheaton, Ill, 2004.

Geisler L. Norman. *If God, Why Evil?* Bethany house publishers: Minneapolis, Minnesota, 2011.

Geisler L. Norman & Zacharias, Ravi. *Who Made God?* Zondervan: Grand Rapids, Michigan, 2003.

Geisler L. Norman. *The Battle for the Resurrection.* Thomas Nelson Publishers. Nashville, Tennessee, 1989.

Greenleaf, Simon. *The Testimony of the Evangelists. The Gospels Examined by the Rules of Evidence Administered in Courts of Justice.* Grand Rapids, Michigan: Kregel, 1995.

Habermas, Gary & Licona R. Michael. *The Case for the Resurrection of Jesus.* Kregel Publications: Grand Rapids, MI, 2004.

Hall John, Douglas. *God & Human Suffering: An exercise in the Theology of the Cross.* Augsburg Publishing House: Minneapolis, 1986. Pg. 118

Harrington, Daniel. *Why do we Suffer? A scriptural approach to the human condition*. Sheed and Ward Publishing: Franklin, Wisconsin, 2000

Hick, John. *Evil and the God of Love*. Macmillan Publishers: Houndsmills, Basing Stroke, Hampshire. First edition 1966. Reprinted with new preface 2010.

Hunter G. Cornelius. *Darwin's God*. Baker Book House: Grand Rapids, Michicigan, 2001.

Joni Eareckson Tada & Steven Estes. *When God Weeps: Why Our Suffering Matter to the Almighty*. Zondervan: Grand Rapids, MI, 1997.

Johnson, Darrel. *Discipleship on the Edge.*

Kaiser C. Walter. *A Biblical Approach to Personal Suffering*. Moody Press: Chicago, Ill, 1982

Keller, Timothy. *The Reason for God*. Riverhead books: 375 Hudson Street, New York, New York, 2008.

Kreeft, Peter. *Making Sense out of Suffering*. Servant Books: Ann Arbor, Michigan, 1986.

Kreef, Peter & Tacelli K. Ronald. *Handbook of Christian Apologetics*. InterVarsityPress: Downers Grove, Ill, 1994

Koukl, Gregory & Beckwith J. Francis. *Relativism: Feet Firmly Planted in Mid Air*. Baker Books: Grand Rapid, Michigan, 1998.

Kushner S. Harold. *When Bad things Happen to Good People*. Anchor Books: New York, NY, 1981.

Lewis, C.S. *The Problem of Pain*. HarperCollins: San Francisco, 1940.

Lewis, C.S. *A Grief Observed*. HarperCollins Publisher: New York, NY, 1961.

Lewis, C.S. *Till We All Have Faces*. HarpeCollins Publisher: New York, NY,

Lewis, C.S. *The Abolition of Man*. HarperCollins: San Francisco, 1974.

Lewis, C.S. *The Magicians Nephew.* HarperCollins Publisher: New York, NY, 1956

Lewis, C.S. *The Last Battle.* HarperCollins Publisher: New York, NY, 1956

Lewis, C.S. *The Screwtape letters.* A Barbour Book: Uhrichsville, OH, 1941.

Lewis, C.S. *Mere Christianity.* HarperCollins: San Francisco, 1942.

Lewis, C.S. *The Four Loves.* HarperCollins Publisher: London, 1960.

Lewis, C.S. *Miracles.* HarpersCollins Publishing: New York, NY, 1960.

Lewis, C.S. *The Poison of Subjectivism: The Collected Works of C.S. Lewis.* Inspirational Press: New York, NY, 1996.

Licona R. Michael. *The Resurrection of Jesus: A New Historiographical Approach.* Intervarsity Press: Downers Grove, Illinois, 2010

Mackie, J.L. *The miracle of Theism.* Oxford University Press: Walton Street, Oxford, 1982.

McDowell, Josh & Sterrett, Dave. *Did the Resurrection happen…really?* Moody Publishers: Chicago, Ill, 2011.

McGrath E. Alister. *Suffering and God.* Zondervan Publishing House: Grand Rapids, Michigan, 1992.

Meyer C. Stephen. *Signature in the Cell.* HarperCollinsPublisher: New York, NY, 2009.

Meyer C. Stephen. *Darwin's Doubt.* HarperCollinsPublisher: New York, NY, 2013

Murray J. Michael. *Nature Red in Tooth and Claw.* Oxford University Press: Great Calrendon Street, Oxford, 2008.

MacAurthor, John. *The Message of the New Testament.* Wheaton, Illinois: Good News, 2005.

Morris Corin, Robert. *Suffering and the Courage of God: Exploring how grace and suffering meet.* Paraclete Press: Brewster, Massachusetts, 2005.

Moreland, J.P. *Scaling the Secular City.* Baker Publishing Group: Grand Rapids, MI, 1987.

Morrison, Frank. *Who Moved the Stone? : A Skeptic Looks at the Death and Resurrection of Jesus.* Zondervan: Grand Rapids, MI, 1930.

Nelson, Kai. *Ethics without God.* Prometheus Books: Amherst, NY, 1990.

Nietzsche, Friedrich. *The Anti-Christ.* Sharp Press: Tucson, AZ, 1999.

Owusu, Sam. *Not Against Flesh and Blood.* DayStreams Publishing: Surrey, BC, 2004

Peterson L. Michael. *God and Evil: An Introduction to the Issues.* Westview Press: Boulder, Colorado, 1998.

Phillips D.Z. *The Problem of Evil & The Problem of God.* Fortress Press: Minneapolis, MN, 2004.

Plantinga, Alvin. *God, Freedom and Evil.* Eerdman's Publishing: Grand Rapids, Michigan, 1974.

Plantinga, Alvin. *God and Other Minds: A Study of the Rational Justification of Belief in God.* Cornell University Press: Ithaca, NY, 1967.

Plantinga, Alvin. *Warranted Christian Belief.* Oxford University Press: New York, NY, 2000.

Russell, Bertrand. *Why I am not a Christian.* Routledge, London, 1957

Stackhouse G. John. *Can God Be Trusted? : Faith and the Challenge of Evil.* InterVarsityPress: Downers Grove, Ill, 2009.

Strobel, Lee. *The Case for Faith.* Zondervan: Grand Rapids, Michigan, 2000.

Strobel, Lee. *The Case for the Real Jesus.* Zondervan: Grand Rapids, Michigan,

2007.

Stott, John. *The Cross of Christ*. Intervarsity Press: Downers Grove, Illinois, 1986.

Swinburne, Richard. *Providence and the Problem of Evil*. Clarendon Press: Oxford, 1998.

Swinburne, Richard. *The Resurrection of God Incarnate*. Clarendon Press: Oxfor, England, 2003.

Swinburne, Richard. *The Evolution of the Soul*. Clarendon Press: Oxford, England, 1986.

Swinburne, Richard. *Is there a God?* Revised Edition. Oxford University Press: Clarendon, Oxford, 1996, 2010.

Sayers L. Dorothy. *"The Greatest Drama ever staged",* in The Whimsical Christian: New York: Collier Macmillan, 1987.

Smart, J.J.C & Williams, Bernard. *Utilitarianism: For and Against*. Cambridge University Press: Cambridge, UK, 1973.

Tchividjian, Tullian. *Glorious Ruin: How Suffering Sets you Free*. Published by David C. Cook: Colorado, CO, 2012.

Walls L. Jerry. *Hell: The Logic of Damnation*. University of Notre Dame Press: Notre Dame, Indiana, 1992.

Wright, N.T. *Evil and the Justice of God*. Downers Grove, Illinois, 2006.

Wright, N.T. *After you Believe: Why Christian Character Matters*. HarperCollins Publisher: New York, NY, 2010.

Wright, N.T. *The New Testament People of God*. Fortress Press: Minneapolis, 1992.

Wright, N.T. *Surprised by Hope*. HarperCollins Publisher: New York, NY, 2008.

Wright, N.T. *The Resurrection of the Son of God.* Fortress Press: Minneapolis, MN, 2003.

Wright, N.T. *The Challenge of Jesus.* InterVarsity Press: Downers Grove, Ill, 1999.

Wright Goring, Nigel. *A Theology of the Dark Side.* Intervarsity Press: Downers Grove, Illinois, 2003.

William Lane Craig & Walter Sinnot - Armstrong. *God ? A Debate Between A Christian and an Atheist.* Oxford University Press: Oxford, New York, 2004.

Wolterstorff, Nicholas. *Lament for a Son.* William B. Eerdman's Publishing Company: Grand Rapids, Michigan, 1987.

Weikert, Richard. *From Darwin to Hitler: Evolutionary ethics, Eugenics, and Racism in Germany.* Palgrave Macmillan: New York, NY, 2004.

Wiesel, Elie. Night. Hill and Wang: New York, NY, 1958.

Vanauken, Sheldon. *A Severe Mercy.* Hodder & Stoughton: Euston Road, London, 1977.

Vermes, Geza. *The Resurrection.* The Doubleday Broadway Publishing Group: New York, NY, 2008.

Yancey, Philip. *The Bible Jesus Read.* ZondervanPublishingHouse: Grand Rapids, MI, 1999.

Yancey, Philip. *Disappointment with God.* ZondervanPublishingHouse: Grand Rapids, Michigan, 1988.

Yancey, Philip. *Where is God when it hurts?* ZondervanPublishingHouse: Grand Rapids, Michigan, 1990.

Made in the USA
San Bernardino, CA
26 February 2014